Soundcloud Rain

John Tucker

chipmunkapublishing
the mental health publisher

Soundcloud Rain

Published by
Chipmunkapublishing
United Kingdom

http://www.chipmunkapublishing.com

John Tucker

@

FIRST THING YOU SEE ON THE BLOGSPOT PAGE: INSERT PHOTOGRAPH OF THE
KITCHEN CLOCK AT THE FOOT OF BLACK COMBE. AROUND MIDNIGHT OR NOON
IT IS HARD TO TELL. THE AUTHOR TOOK IT BECAUSE IT WAS ONCE CONTENDED
"A CLOCK IS ONLY AS FAST AS CHEETAH" BY THE AUTHOR AS A SEVEN YEAR
OLD CHILD.

2: PAGE TWO

INSERT A SECOND
COVER PHOTOGRAPH ON
THE BLOGSPOT PAGE:

THE SHEET WHERE
PICTURES BROWN
AND BLUE SIMPLY GREW:

AS DISCOVERED BY THE
AUTHOR UPON THE PASSING
OF HIS FATHER

MR. GILES ADRIAN
GRICE TUCKER

LOVING HUSBAND
AND FATHER

REST IN PEACE.

John Tucker

BONUS TRACK: THE DEATH OF ROCK N ROLL

Di di dit di di dit di di dit dit dit
Di di dit di di dit di di dit dit dit
Di di dit di di dit di di dit dit dit

Bring bring
bring bring

"Hello?"

Gold member, you're the one,
the one with the heart of gold

Vowels, pure vowels
Immanuel Kant
will come to thee
with immanence

You come home smacked up you come

d/ d/ d/ down
grooving up slowly

d/ d/ d/ down
grooving up slowly

d/ d/ d/ down
grooving up slowly

yeah yeah yeah
yeah yeah yeah
yeah yeah yeah

boom
boom
boom
boom
boom

how did we get down here from flat-top
wide tunnel cities self driving cars
bears in the moon and liquor and drugs
and whisky baaaaaaaaaaaars

boom shanka, you're the one,
the one with the sonic boom

Soundcloud Rain

knickers knickers faster than lightning

skin up fall out of bed

and did those feet
in ancient times

rain down, rain down,
come on raindown
and walk the sun

fatter, hippier, less well connected

always walk the hallways
down to create my own
and in the meantime
and in the meantime
I'll do the monkey bars with my legs

manic depression has enraptured my name
don't know what I want but I just want shame
don't know what I want but I just won't shave

rainy waif, rain always,
lay back and dream
on a rainy waif

now I know how Kurt Cobain sang
oh now I know how Kurt Cobain sang
no more laaaaaaaaaa la's

removal van canes will be turned into furniture
we're thinking of putting Tricky's name on the front sir
you never see me dead near an inch of closure

|| | |||| | || | |||| 909 and 693 are wings

"and a record made of sound
goes round and round, conveying
music to the speaker through the stylus,"
says the radio as I turn it on.

Well, although there is no
such thing as the Nirvana barcode
it opens up a discussion about
the Telepathic Walkie Talkie, how
if barcode is rain barcode is phone...

and at least I have
the grace to come
back and say that the
extinction of consciousness

has no monetary value.

It is past dawn
and I see that
that first mobile
phone has gone.

SAIL AWAY

I know it may sound like it's none of your business but the first time I voted Labour it was because the song 'Sail Away' was on in the background or even the foreground of the village hall where we vote.

- Anon

John Tucker

INTRODUCTION

This book is a book of songs. First of all you have the words to a record by The Flood which is recorded through earphones, binaural earphones, I tell you, with tiny mics implanted inside them. Then we have four solo albums. The solo work is organised according to the new Da Vinci circle, which is like a cyclical pattern designed by my brother Mr. James P D Tucker that goes as follows

<BEE>   [long squiggle]

Infinity Symbol

Although I don't understand it fully, I would say the above quote represents my brother's experiment into the international language alphabet; and it has certainly influenced and inspired the naming and organisation of the four solo albums. Then there is also room for a brief mention of some of my work with Grant Aspinall that followed on from The Flood. Unused and unrecorded songs are also included herein.

'BEHIND ENEMY LINES' BY THE FLOOD

John Tucker

On the day his A-level results came through at his little school up north John – who had written the highest marked English Literature A-level exam essay in the nation - went down south to stay with Paul and to look for work.

Their plan was to earn enough to join John's Finnish grandfather on his home-made yacht in the Caribbean. John's Finnish grand-father had built his own steal hull yacht in his back garden upon retiring and was now sailing round the world. John and his friend Paul were supposed to work and earn enough to join him for their Gap Year.

Instead they formed a band who soon began to record an album only through state-of-the-art, binaural earphones, which meant earphones with tiny, tiny mics implanted inside them. The album they made was more of an algorithm than an album, contained very few words and on it John promised to plug his senses in the mains.

Soundcloud Rain

I

HUNGER

(by The Flood and now online)

I e I e I e have I e I e I e have
I e I e I e have I have Hunger
I'm a sick magnet I e I e I e I'm in want
maybe all I need is a new pair of shades
I'm a craving slave for you
your pleasure's dust your pleasure's just
your pleasure's just your suffering's bait
it's a sucker's fate for you
escape escape escape escape
your home your clothes and all you know
leave no footprint in the snow it's just a photo
escape escape escape your name
your stain your skin your dead routine
for the pristine dream for her
I'm going to get your freshness back
plug my senses in the mains
it's just a bloodrush to my brains
I'm going to get pretty much f***ed up
flee this world on a midnight plane
dance with the aliens and the insane.

II

VOODOO ECHO   13

(by the Flood and recorded through earphones]

Well, I say this number is by The Flood but at one point I am massacring Jimi Hendrix which seems looking back to be folly to me now. The best bit about this song is that we – or rather I - through patience and spontaneity alike – manage to incorporate as much feedback and static as is possible onto the binaural earphone album, where this number goes in at number 2. Credit to Tommo for naming the song especially considering he wasn't even playing on this number! Such a thing is typical of the Flood's modus operandi.

III

THE WARNING

(recorded through state of the art binaural earphones in The Flood and now online)

Going to meet with the Otherness,
best go get a party dress,
play a stone, live in the wilderness,
I'm going to beat with the Otherness.

Suddenly their brain is an alien visitation,
suddenly I am the imposter againe,
lying in secret wait of myself,
knife ready to treat the pain.

IV

F # MINOR

Well, this is an instrumental by the Flood, which was recorded through earphones in the middle of the night in Cambridgeshire. Wolf aka Agent G (who procured the earphones from his bro and was our drummer) came up with this weird detuning (we were always detuning guitars) and h-a-n-d-e-d me the guitar, whereupon I jammed around for a bit until I knew what I was doing then I said "right I'm ready" and Tommo was on bass and Agent G on drums and we recorded this number, this instrumental jam which is said to be the Flood's best song, one where we got the cat from Piper just right. I mean what is the street-name for the drug 'Ecstasy' when you start to detune the guitar strings all the way? For me, F sharp minor is the answer to that question… and the point this song is trying to make. Whether or not Agent G knew that when he handed me the guitar in the F Sharp minor detuning I cannot say – but I would not put it past him. I cannot even say if I knew it when Tommo later asked me what the song was called and I said "F Sharp Minor." Whatever the case it seems an almost unbearably beautiful piece and especially so for having something behind the words. I would also like to say that in The Flood we kind of posited the idea that O is the key of water and its soul-assuaging sound, and that is beautiful too – so all told we had a lot going on. When voices later told me to lose the book or the guitar, maybe there was already no choice by then.

V

MANTRA OF A MADMAN

(by The Flood and recorded thru' binaural earphones!)

Well, I was going to say this number has no words but that would be a lie. It has one line, a mantra. I inverted the Great I Can, I Am from Venice Beach, 1967 into the mantra "I Am, I can," because it had to be that way round for the earphones. Paul and I are singing it in major harmonies, and it's said to be one of the most beautiful moments on a very beautiful record. I say record but my feelers are out and my Google search engines are primed and bring back news that what we had was actually an algorithm more than an album!

John Tucker

VI

THE BLASTS

[by The Flood and recorded through earphones]

[The Blasts has no words it is a bad monkey funky prog rock or even math rock rhythm and riff sequence I wrote when I was living in the shed and the song goes on at the end of our little record a beautiful record that contains six of the best this one being the sixth for all it starts with plugging the senses in the mains and we have six of them if you include as Professor Morley says thanatos I. e. an increasing sense of one's own mortality in life as the perceptual kingdom of the individual enters overdrive.]

This is where I wrote a song called Space Is Big, which should if I had stayed follow on in the album or algorithm. In fact there were many, many other songs, and some of them recordings, that didn't make it to the algorithm. Anyhow, let's say I never went home – was never kicked out the band for weird behaviour – never came back to the north and got a mature students' degree interrupted by mental illness before a full-on diagnosis.

John Tucker

PHOTOGRAPH THREE:

**INSERT PHOTOGRAPH OF THE
TAPE I COOKED IN THE AGA
WHEN ITS PAUSE IN THE
OPENING SONG WHERE
CUT AND RESEALED IN
THE REEL SOMEHOW
HEALED AND WAS GONE**

Soundcloud Rain

ACKNOWLEDGEMENTS

Thanks to all the musicians I ever played with including James Tucker, Robert Tucker, Hannah Tucker, Alick and Steve from Oedipus Wrecks, Rohan, Ed Green, Ben Fridja, Will Fenn, Tom Fitzgerald, Paul Inman, Zach Lait, Dobbin, Tom Barham, Steve Adams, Niki Galan, Tom Woodhall, Mark Velarde, Jez Williams, Max Bondi, John Duckitt, Mike Eccleshall, John Gray, Simon Pomery, Grant Aspinall, Colin, Martin, and more and many more. Yeah.

John Tucker

RECORDING NOTES FROM DR. ROBERT

1) Install the audio interface - https://www.youtube.com/watch?v=UGoQLfrW0nk

2) Make sure it's enabled - https://help.ableton.com/hc/en-us/articles/115000204630-Setting-up-ASIO4ALL-Windows-

3) Add the audio interface to Ableton - https://youtu.be/D9tjzSctp_Q

4) Record - https://www.youtube.com/watch?v=7PbmTaJopec

How to record

Step 1: |Make sure that the audio interface is plugged in BEFORE starting Ableton. After opening Ableton, check your correct driver is enabled. Options > preferences > audio .

Driver type = Asio
Audio Device = Asio 4 All v 2

If you click on "hardware setup" you should see both "realtek" (this is the soundcard that comes with the laptop) and TI PCM2902 (this is the Behringer). Click on the power icon to disable realtek and enable the Behringer.

Step 2: Go from session view (the DJ view) to arrangement view (this is the wide view that is more suitable for those doing long recordings). To do this hit tab.

Step 3: Make sure the sound is coming through from the guitar. Click on any track that is of type audio (i.e. not midi). Note that each track goes horizontally and represents a different instrument. When you click on the track a white flashing cursor will appear. This means that you will begin recording from this place. Then click on the "record enable" button for that track. Each track has a dropdown which is set to Ext. In by default. Ext. In is the correct option. If the guitar is plugged in to the left hand channel on the Behringer (where the mic goes) then channel 1 should be selected. Channel 2 corresponds to the second channel on your Behringer. You can see the sound coming in on the audio channel you selected on the far right hand side.

Step 4: Click on the record button that is located near the top of the page to begin recording.

22

'THE NEW BEAT' BY JOHN F B TUCKER

I

John Tucker

DREAM WITH OPEN EYES

(by Secret Chord H originally and used as radio jingle circa 1999)

Last night it seemed we couldn't
sleep but maybe I was dreaming.
The world expands inside my
hands it's getting heavy.

Of all the treasures I could
choose I can't seem to decide.
Today the shade was washed
away where I would hide.

Dream with open eyes, come
below and we can fantasise.
Now that I've stopped telling lies, come
below and we can fantasise.

Last night it seemed we nearly
died but maybe I was dreaming.
It made me feel soooooooooooooo
alive and soooooooo in love.

II

CHOCOLATE DOG

MY DOG HAS GOT NO BRAIN/ MY DOG IS A TOTAL PAIN/ HE'S GOT THREE EYES /
AND A BIG FAT NOSE / AND GETS HIMSELF TANGLED / WITH THE GARDEN HOSE/
HE ONCE TOOK A PILL / THAT MADE HIM ILL/ AND EVER SINCE THEN/ HE'S BEEN
STANDING VERY STILL.

III

John Tucker

BAD DAY AT THE OFFICE

Such a bad day at the office
down the pub to get pissed
though I can't afford it
we'll never get a pay rise

stay up till sunrise
call in sick in the morning
spend the whole day mourning
underneath the covers

where the fuck is Batman
Sugar Candy Mountain
waiting for some action
heard it brings good fortune

papers want a scandal
tell them the truth
if you can handle
what a fucking headline

where in Hell is Tinkerbell
somewhere alone and dying
dawn calls in sick in the morning
what's the use in trying

don't believe in dying
it's shocking and appalling
it's four o'clock in the morning
and Paradise is boring.

IV

CHIEF OF THE BLACKBIRD SPIES

Well I fell up a sycamore tree
and nearly spilled my glass of wine,
and though nobody came for me
I didn't mind it I felt fine,

for I was trading stories
w/ the chief of the black bird spies
amongst new leaves and old branches
that don't know how to tell lies...

He said to forget the job,
sack the boss, and hang the cage
which containeth all your rage
for but the minimum wage.

I said it's easy for you
in your neighbouring Otherness -
be Nature custodial or frightening? -
to avoid the mad enemy Stress.

He said he finds it fun-loving
to tense-hop all around
for cataclysm is catalyst for the cat
that sat on the map of sound.

Quite soon he spread his wings
until his wings were spread
and flew to Morrisons supermarket
for a tamed and manner'd head.

He'd said he thinks privation
is the mother of imagery,
and inconsiderate violation
at the root of the creation of beauty.

We'd bemoaned a lost society
w/ all its malaise and cheap talk,
its word-ways no better than
cheep cheep squawk squawk.

We'd spoken in no uncertain terms
and out in the great outdoors
where Mother Nature operates
according to her natural laws.

When he left it grew quite quiet
for he was a tremendous talker
and had a way with words

and had said I would go far…

when I left his sycamore tree
I was glad to see my own home
and return to my own kind
near the beach that's full of foam

but I remembered that black bird
and his eloquent influence
performing from the end of a branch
in ways that just made sense.

V

SYMMETRY LIPS

Symmetry lips	symmetry lips
kiss me quicks	need a fix
make me feel	natural and real
cuts heal	with a plastic seal
I've been in your heart	and danced in hot rain
I've been in your heart	and danced in hot rain
now consciousness	is everywhere
now consciousness	is sentient air
the sky falls	apart into place
I crave to sleep	behind your face
everything in its	proper place
live where the sky	and the river freely give
live where the sky	and the river freely give

VI

AIR RAID SHELTER 29

(originally recorded through state of the art binaural earphones in The Flood but not used for
their record)

Air raid shelter, we're in it together,
let's not get entrenched too deeply,
fear and pain's our only motivation,
got to break free from that habit apathy.

Clinging to loveless, sweaty, rubber limbs
won't cure your heart, it's a painful art,
air-raid shelter, we're in it together now,
wrap me away in your wombs and duvets.

See this world from outer space minor,
saaaaaaaaafe distances have found
all our solid, common ground,
echo grammanon habeo amore.

Won't your spaceships come to find me,
pull myself right back to the centre,
attack on all sides, hold you soooooo tight
now that there is noooooo time.

I'm just trying to forget how to smell acid,
and still it seems acid isn't flaccid,
but I think that you'll find I still
got there in the end somehow.

VII

THE NEW BEAT

Door the case fluff the line feel the last dull the white hone the drift dawn the most deaf the ear grope the bread fee the seat blue the ticket dream the lemon boat the weed I watched myself today in postures of raw decay because there was nothing else to do mine the brick dwarf the vote peace the bull D the random renew the two widen the road steal the wings gate the lane mean the scene send the head rend the Hell roll the ball I watched myself today in postures of raw decay because there was nothing else to do visual radio was on in the car and bike and train and bus and lorry and van visual radio was on in the boat and tractor and plane and train and truck

(C/ Em/ G/ F/ G/ C)

John Tucker

VIII

LUCY IN THE SOUL WITH DEMONS

I no longer know if Lucy in the soul with demons
even happens to be an actual substance

but I know that acid can alter personality
and when home-made and strong be very scary.

Do not flinch at your own shadow when
you take its dark receipt into the glen

for panic in a wild stallion horse's eye
can spread like wild-fire across the madding sky

where a digital wind of blue and green
blows in fake and chemical as glycerine

and the derangement of the senses can go
hang its head in shame, dear Master neo-Rimbaud.

IX

PRIVATE DETECTIVES AND SECRET SPIES

I sleep in a hole for the Hoover tonight
there's always something not quite right
look at a wall it's not too hard to see
all the cracks and flaws beneath the paint
maybe all we need is to decorate the place
private detectives and secret spies
seem to have uncovered all of my lies,
scars and birthmarks beneath my skin,
should I sever my face with razor blades
to show you some ugly truth w/in
well maybe I should but I'd prefer to
score your flawless body with sin
like two new humans made for life
with default buttons to wipe any slate clean
and one of them man and one of them wife
in Crufts as it is in the black angel's death song

X

John Tucker

A SMALL ADVERT FOR FREE SEX

My name is David Bonky,
I'm a knock-kneed hummingbird,
there's a tear up my jacket
and I heard a magic word:
Trans/ philo/ quis/ ation.
I fly through colours and shapes.
Lightspeed is my passport.
The countries are for apes.
A knock-kneed hummingbird
table on which to land and read
does not seem to me to be
such an unreasonable need.
I'll breakfast on snooker
colours, spark a dullard cigarette,
sail the wind of change and
have no room for regret.
I deem it quite Romantic
to go do the monkey bars
with my legs into her open
chamber underneath the stars.
I think love is both the all-
seeing eye and love is blind.
So wear an emotional condom
before you fuck my mind.
For that's what language is,
the emotional condom of
the world into which we're
all thrown in search of love.
Soon I must fly on, from
this gnarled treefinger perch,
and heal the glitch in the soul,
and join the Giant Search.
I don't know what we're
searching for but it'll find us first.
Maybe just some peace and
quiet to slake the eternal thirst.

XI

THE POWER-BALLAD OF MARTIN VICIOUS

I can see death and see flippers
coming out of his senses and say
"come closer you f***ing terrorist,
come closer you f***ing terrorist,
come closer you f***ing terrorist."
It's because I live a life of all time leisure,
all drugs pure and the radiance just right.
I might be wrong but then I might.
Score some dodgy crack and die
here alone with nobody for a name.
I can be Proust and fathom ten
or eleven types of ambiguity and
rue them all cantankerously,
rue them all cantankerously,
rue them all cantankerously.
It's because I live a dream of my still
working, all love pure and trust in the night.
I might be wrong but then I might.
Score some dodgy crack and die
here alone with nobody for a name.

John Tucker

XII

OCEANS SMILE

(originally by Oedipus Wrecks)

Oceans smile with liquid eyes
and fill themselves with rain.
The tide goes out and leaves me
stranded, the last thing a glass gene.
Follow me to the resurrection
while the blind get crucified.
My weapon's only loaded in my eyes.

Death will come on silky wings
but I for one will not go.
A soul is endless, oceans severed
and keeeeeeeps a perfect O.
Follow me to the resurrection
while the blind get crucified.
My weapon's only loaded in my eyes.

Go drink the ocean with your tea
cup, give your heart far out.
If oceans smile with liquid eyes
then they'll give you a shout.
Follow me to the resurrection
while the blind get crucified.
My weapon's only loaded in my eyes.

Too drunkenly I sail the water
on Rimbaud's smoking boat.
With whiskygills primed in fire
I sail the waves to Boot.
Follow me to the resurrection
while the blind get crucified.
My weapon's only loaded in my eyes.

(reconstructed via the new, synchronised word)

Well, the boiler man is coming and I have to give mum a shout when he arrives. The guys in The Flood met my mum down there by the way. They called her. They called her down. It was a case of my own weird behaviour having unsettled them I think. What bothered the guys was when I came home from the pub with Tommo after having had 3 "F sharp minors," 5 White Russians and then we started to puff green whom it would seem was always there and I launched into a speech in an imaginary language, ad-libbing it, impromptu, keeping it up for half an hour while rolling on the floor in the professional hysterics of neo-shamanism until they thought they had lost me completely whereupon I went to the shed and had sex with the cold concrete floor on ecstasy – or tried to. That was why they called my mum and said I had been behaving very strangely. So I had to go home after all we'd done and went off to get a degree from my local University (Lancaster), deeming it a word-guitar from Fender. Half way through the weirdest things started to happen – visions and voices and electric semen flying around and holograms and projections and special effects and books changing and body parts seeming to as well and you name it – and I was hospitalised. I still got my degree after a 28 lie down but have been on heavy meds ever since. Now I sit and wait for the boiler man to arrive – here at the fell foot which has been visited by the way by the guys, in The Flood, whom it would seem I kind of miss. Only yesterday did I have my depot – which means an anti-psychotic injection – and I haven't slept since then because I am eager to get a good book out there…

John Tucker

37

'SONGS IN G' BY JOHN F B TUCKER

Soundcloud Rain

I

BONECHINA DRUM

Where has all my washing gone?
Maybe it has gone to Heaven!
Mirrors on the street rebound.
Everyone is happy and free.

My dream-meet experiment tended there.
Not the local DogMuckels.
All walks of life were gathered and one.
To wake from the dream is to die.

That's when you put on your socks.
Unless they've gone into the sock void.
Don't mind me I'm paranoid.
I've got some bizarre ideas.

If a clock is only as fast as a cheetah
I. T. might stand for Instant Travel
but I'll pad downstairs and drink a cup
only at my own slow speed.

II

FLOWER-PRESS LOVE POEM MUSIC

If a flower-press ending on cannabis
could seem to equal a dialysis
then a love poem hoping to impress Flora
could seem to equal more a motor

but giving up weed in order to be free
I can't see how this really matters to me
and if it's a system I just love you still
and love has not gone under the green hill

if all the noise in the world would be quiet
I'd hide in the cupboard during the riot
if systems rule with fear not love
I'd half it and laugh it with an imperfect dove

here I am at the foot of Sea Ness
this anagram of boredom is in a mess
I'm all set up for a walk on the beach
to watch the waves rolling out of my reach

I trust my family and I trust my friends
I hope my dog's life never quite ends
the kitchen is clean because I cleaned it myself
my father's philosophy is up on the shelf

if all the greed in the world would go away
I'd still be Bede at the end of the day
if power is wrong at least it's transient
a birthday came and a birthday went

and this is the me we all want to see
and this is the way I know to be free
and this is the Now that is in Eternity
and this is the leaf that came to the tree

if the wording of this little contract is mine
alas you are not but I'm still feeling fine
I've seen the stars that are out tonight
I've tried to forget exactly what colour is white

I'm drifting to E on the end of a stick
I'm searching my memory but it's just a block
if only I could hold you in my arms
I've fallen for all your loquacious charms

Soundcloud Rain

III

ICARUS UNBOUND

(a finger-picker in the drone of G)

I really love you my friend Mark,
don't get me wrong I am not gay,
it's just a way for me to start,
it's just something to say…

placing bets on raindrops running
down the opaque window pane,
I have been a melting robot,
then they said I was insane…

there you are across the water,
living on the Isle of Man,
if only my attention-span could
be more like Peter Pan…

you're the one who taught me de-tunings,
stairs down to The Velvet Underground,
I am the one in love with Flora,
and that fertile map of sound…

you say it's got too late to make it,
I hear you crawl through new air,
but I was never one to fake it,
I for one don't really care…

in your room was a very high ceiling
and I remember it was bright,
I can almost taste the loving feeling,
even though now it is Night…

you could not tell if the vocal
in Aphex Twin was a demon
so made us listen to Nick Drake when
on another easy comedown…

lines are blurred in drug-slurred idiom.
lyrical streaks now open up.
I'm thinking of youth which has now flown.
but I've still got a little plastic cup.

John Tucker

IV

THE FIRE-DANCE   41

The fire-dance dwelled in electric drums
where ecstasy fell soft fathoms to clap
and bells let peace form in blue notes
and peered at beer in the wood and ate of it
and wet let excellence sound out its criticism
and dawn let sting its unsheathed sting
and chloroform in the heart let see
if only Game Over was seen in nights.

V

THE GREEN BLUES

I read through the news,
hats off to your blues,
a chimney falls under my head.

I stomach the wood
that tastes very good,
like mopping up gravy with bread.

I glow for the coal,
don't bury your soul,
backwards in spire I get high.

I'd change for the house
that's quiet as a mouse
and emblazon my name in the sky.

I'd slip through the skin
of a thesis as thin
as the Rizla it's in and be born.

I'd light it and write it,
I'd burn and unlearn,
I'd even hairdress the dawn.

I'd sip on White Russians,
on white and South African,
and amble to 360 vision.

To take out my eyes and
see in all directions at once
is but one general direction.

VI

SONG OF THE NEON DAWN

X-ray specs don't lead to sex
and mobile phones don't have gay undertones
and television is a big decision
and the internet can't just forget

and laser beams are born in dreams
and digital clocks don't come in flocks
and Ableton Live is my nine to five
and the latest App is an angel's lap

and I sing for Kate whose always late
and I write the Night until it's white
and my vertigo lives down below
and my neon dawn will be reborn

and we'll renew the morning dew
and Google our senses out there like a tide
and dream of love aloft on wings
and try and forget the nights we cried

and the alphabet is the suicide note
of Nelly the Elephant if you deem it true
and love's gone veggie over Disney again
and the grass is green and the sky is blue

and E is a bet with the myriad mind
and I've seen so much I've gone blind
and a poem's a seat where you sit and eat
and a driverless car has gone quite far

and a use for dust is a beautiful bust
and the wheel of a bike is a map of the Lakes
and a rugby match is quite a catch
and an abandoned band is written in the sand

and a red skin cell is a state of Hell
and sadness seems the mother of dreams
but maybe that's the other way round
and a flower grows just for your nose

VII

BIRTHDAY OF I. A.

You're not a knock-kneed hummingbird, / you're not a birthday of I. A, / and who you are I'll never know now, / and if I did I'd never say… / I am your med-banging elephantine, / and I cry on the windows of trains, / and maybe all I need's a length of, / need's a length of metal chain… / and through it all I wish you rainbows, / made for two and very strange, / and somehow what's most familiar, / is what really can estrange you, / rearrange and slowly derange you, / oh yes it most definitely can. / So don't run in the corridor / or you'll sin in the eyes of Santa / as he watches on.

VIII

TELEPATHIC ELEPHANT 45

Another, another, another fucking joint.
Another, another, another fucking joint.
Another, another, another fucking joint.
Another, another, another fucking joint.
Another, another, another fucking joint.
Another, another, another fucking joint.
Another, another, another fucking joint.
Another, another, another fucking joint.
Another, another, another fucking joint.

[Note: this song which was originally a Secret Chord H B-side concerns a Pearl Jam 'VS' cassette tape with a pause in the opening number where the reel is cut and re-sealed. In a sense it is about healing the pause in the song and then cooking the object in the dark blue AGA, top oven, hottest one.]

IX

THE SWITCH THROWN

Blessed may be the end at last
under the sea
below the soul
in the upside-down
Oceans above us

(all that heaven sends is rain)

and blessed is the rain that heaven sends
it is the life for the gilly flowers
some might say
it even falls up
and you're going to have to think againe

for a clock's only as fast
as a wounded cheetah
who knows how to
get drunk on cold Wifebeater
but gets drunk instead
on the rhythm and metre

O love thanks
for coming round,
O love cherish
your map of sound,
O love I dreamt that
we were drowned

I made such a mess it's wasn't cool
but at least I didn't
give it away
that music is
the sacred pool
or whatever else I had to say

it's half past four but then again
the Night is young
the switch is thrown
whatever could
the poor boy mean
he means his heart is yours to own

X

SAD HYPOCHONDRIAC

I know she's only a phone call away...
maybe she's got something to say?
Anyway by now her number's probably changed...
seems even numbers can't just stay the same.

You always used to say to me
"to love someone truly is to set them free" -
you always knew better than me
you always knew better than me.

I know she's only a daydream away -
transient rainbow not made to stay -
only made of sunlight and tears! -
beauty like that should last for years.

You always used to say to me
"to love someone truly is to set them free" -
you always knew better than me
you always knew better than me.

I'm just a sad hypochondriac.
Just another shooting rock star in love with the black.
Don't want to die of a sudden art attack.
I'm just a sad hypochondriac.

I'm just a sad hypochondriac.
I'm just a sad hypochondriac.
I'm just sorry for everything I lack.
I'm just a sad hypochondriac.

XI

Soundcloud Rain

WE COULD BE SO HAPPY

(played at a gig on a rooftop in London, the last gig by The Flood)

Serotonin dopamine
no Codeine or Diazepam
I got ruin'd you got wrecked
let's just say yes to each other's plans
we could be so ha ha ha happy
we could be so ha ha ha happy
Buproprion and Fluoxetine
a toooooooootal loss of all
language-is-thought-control
it's just some sedative we'll
hide away under snow
I wake up dying for some
junk food to save my hole
when all the money has run out
and our housing contract expires
and the pigs come to track us down
the night will be filled with burning fires
the night will be filled with screeching tyres
the night will be filled with burning lyres
we could be so ha ha ha happy
in the future that ain't what it used to be
on a drug called Strictly Free
on the loss of the cannabis battery.

John Tucker

49

'THE WHITE DOOR' BY JOHN F B TUCKER

I

HEARTBOOK

We'll never take E on a green,
Glastonbury hillside ever again,
never see Love playing through dark,
aviator Ray-Bans after the rain,
we'll never be young as we once were
and looking back I know it's all gone,
the real E's a she and she is not free,
but we can converse while you're on a plane

flying over the Atlantic ocean
you message me online full of emotion
to say new material has emerged

I tell you've never done anything
which you need to apologise to me for,
you kept me in food when in Berlin
I spent my last money on a whore,
Everything happened back in the day
and we isolate bits to form a narrative,
everything that is except for work,
and we used to say live and let live

flying over the Atlantic ocean
you message me online the ball still in motion
to say new evidence has emerged

If work sets you free I will never feel
freedom not like I did back in the day,
the day we were young, you and me
playing in the band, whatever we used to play,
and only the songs seem to survive,
the poems don't seem to want to last,
and I'm trying to learn Ableton Live,
and get your message like a blast from the past

flying over the Atlantic ocean
you text me online w/ a true notion
to say unheard music by us has emerged

II

John Tucker

TRUE LOVE DOT COM

Dead clock plodding play a different song // we're waiting for some action and some change to come along // been waiting all night at true love dot com // you're only just starting to notice the mushrooms are still too strong // dead pedestrians thinking fumes stay in and get fat in your new chat rooms // we chase the wave forms of the dusky dawn w/ black shadow cat-prints going backwards on the lawn // and I confess my open heart is lying w/ her legs apart // and if she said she's in love w/ me I wouldn't go taking it personally // for love has no ego as everybody knows and something inside me she's given me grows // and a playground swing on the vexed edge of life sighs empty and forever and out falls a leaf // and not into love does that green leaf fall where wet Westerly winds swoop and call // we are the glitter on the Christmas trees and not the litter in the filibustering breeze // and the E comedown has no value in maths // and the loonies all walk on the wrong paths // and the grass is green on the Other Side // it pulls the ropes of the evening tide.

III

THE SUPERSTRING GUITAR

Cool white is the highnote if it's up to me,
cascading down to the deep blue sea -

will blue trousers over the trouser blues
fall down on the Excellent News?

Music penetrates is-ness,
renovates sensation's quest.

Out in the desert the pigeon-stars
ripe w/ new creatures won't bring out the Tsars.

Water splits but the desert's dry.
Stonemouth silence chewing gums by.

Why the high note seems to be white
is the sideways gravity in the smile of night.

The Super String Guitar was electric and was smashed.
Transcendence is the dream of anything squashed.

"You're going to get a dog w/ a laser brain."
L to the pregnant snorkel = mc squared.

Impairing the wild pear tree to tears.
Impairing the wild pear tree to pears.

Flutter in the sideways gravity of the smile of light.
Phew for a minute there you lost the screen.

E = L to the pregnant snorkel.
E = L to the pregnant snorkel.

L to the pregnant snorkel = mc squared.
Flutter in the sideways gravity of the smile of light.

John Tucker

IV

BAXTER

I love my dog
he's barking mad
when he wants to smile
he wags his tail
his uncomplicated love
is healing for the soul
he has seventy words
like the book with smell
I wonder what the others are
maybe later I'll know
mashed potato and stew
and a Pizza Hut
and the waves of the sea
go round and round
swim in mystery
but do not drown
ice cream is nice
on Freedom's shore
so is sugar and spice
and more and many more
and so it came to pass
that I sat in a room
with the dog by my side
and the music on
and I've got the dog blues
yeah I've got the dog blues
which only means
I've nothing to lose
and the stream of life
flows on and on
and a cup of tea
awaits in the kitchen
and the dream of love
has not quite died
and I feel assured
deep down inside
because I love my dog
he loves me too
what more do I need
don't need to sniff glue
to feel all high
when I have fresh air
and the Emperor has
abdicated againe
and a nice long sleep
will reunite me
with planet earth

at the end of the day
what more can I say

John Tucker

V

FAREWELL TO THE SEER OF SEA NESS

Farewell to the seer of Sea Ness -
see you later when the future is less.
What will you do about your trance?
Will you send a postcard from France?
I hope that you have a lot of fun…
I hope that you may find someone -
and the scenery streams by the train
and the world is small beneath the plane

Farewell to the seer of Sea Ness -
see you in the future when the past is less.
Will the future there be quite cold?
Will you feel sad and feel old?
I hope that your dreams all come true.
I hope that there's hope for you too -
and the dreams stream beside the car -
and you make it Westwards quite far.

Farewell to the seer of Sea Ness -
see you in the light we might bless.
Will the visual radio still swirl?
Will you still blame it on the girl?
I hope that your heart will beat on…
I hope that your hope's not all gone -
and the freedom you find is the best,
and the beauty you dream is a quest.

Farewell to the seer of Sea Ness -
see you in the middle released from the stress.
Will the sound of silence be heard?
Will they hide the mystic bird?
I hope that your love arrows down.
I hope that you don't hit the brown -
and the light will puncture you
and the good life will still be true.

VI

THE GHOSTS LAMENT (THE GUZZLER MEN)

(Oedipus Wrecks)

I'm the only one left, left to shoot my
own gun. This is the dead land. Crack a smile
and curse the sun. Death awaits to fuck me.
Give me bliss and give me kisses. Death a-
waits to save me. The ghosts lament, the ghosts
lament. Come on baaaaaaaaaby, you know it's e-
asy, don't say maaaaaaaaaybe, let's go crazy. Death
awaits to fuck me. Give me bliss and give
me kisses. Death awaits the same me. The
ghosts lament, the ghosts lament, no more ghosts.

[Note: when I discovered the James P D Tucker sheet where pictures grew, and the pictures
seemed to depict the lyric to one of my old songs, this is the song.]

VII

THAT BLACK NATURAL E

[spoken word narrative for B minor]

Where once I wandered far and wide
on a field-file, a file-field,
a fenceless farm without
security alarm where all hearts bleed
and all arts breed, now Hell
is very quiet, unadvertised.

McBreastmilk,
McBreastmilk,
don't feed your kids.

Gentle face erasing cream,
smear it in and let it sink
down through the pores of your skin
to erase your deepest down dirt.

O stars the government
that truly speaks for us!

Get an extra kid for free
when you spend 99p.

Freefall 0800 down
your own black hole pupils.

Maybelline you maybe only make-believe
you may be the true mating queen of the hive,
may mad vampires stalk you,
stalking walls walk through
your vagrant dreams.

I see state of head
is more than Head of State.

Monster Munch can
always gobble up your food.

Cancerel can always
sweeten the stewed-
carfume coffee we sip in
this liminal afterlounge.

It's getting cramped
as a tin of beans in here.

Soundcloud Rain

In emergency please
break glass and exit.

Credits at the end of innocence
are falling like numberless lists
of fallen autumn leaves.

Snatched handfuls of light
come to nothing in the dark room.

There must be a use for
this dust amounting.

There's nothing like digging
a meaningless hole as if to cure the
spiralling lethargy of Hell...

and when I went into the
woods to bury my soul,
all the trees knelt down.

O perpetual orgasm of the sun!

Privation is the mother of imagery.

Prayers, ghosts and
e-mails chatter on
the ego-loss breeze.

The chitchat in the solipsistic
kitchen of fiction is 'phatic'.

My new, motley fridge magnet
letters contain no question
mark in the pack but the first
qualification of Modernism
is enquiry and furthermore
wilful ignorance is a sin.

Meanwhile outside the
fallen Autumn leaves
are where bears have
dipped their feet in pots of paint
and danced across the threshold
of the paving stones.

Water clears its throat from the tap.

Gunpowder was only invented
for fireworks and a firework
is a champion sperm nosing up

blind to explode bright and wonderful
deep-sea creatures in the Ancient Night.

The world is a cool, bejewell'd
marble snug in Holy Orbit
suckling on a mother sun.

Supposedly there is soon
to be New Atlantis on the moon.

The cure for cancer
sustains your heart.

Robbed by a bastard vending machine,
somewhere a tramp drinks paint-stripper
to cleanse the doors of perception,
a drunkard attacks a wall
on an otherwise empty street,
a policeman forces himself
to come with a gun.

Hey salesman
slow down
with that
fast-food.

I don't mind
waiting here
for a year.

(2002)

VIII

WAVETABLE IN C

I remember when my mnemonic for the guitar strings was Even A Dick Gets Big Erections…
now I don't need one, I've heard a better one from a fellow autist, high-functioning autist –
Even A – no – er - Every Acid Dealer Gets Busted Eventually. At the moment I'm on James' red
electric. I remember when he got it for Christmas and I got an acoustic, a Fender, an expensive
one, and I wanted to be Kurt Cobain so I was annoyed that I got an acoustic not an electric. I
was upset and offended my parents. And now here I am playing on James' red electric. As I say
my mnemonic used to be Even A Dick Gets Big Erections, but this one's in C. I'll leave it up to
you to work out what that means. Your guess is as good as mine. It could be for countryside. It
could be for court case. It could be for caliphate. It could be for civilisation. It could be for
completion of the soul.

John Tucker

IX

NO DEATH ONLY CHANGE

Don't be afraid/ there is no death only change/ let's pretend, let's pretend/ there is no end of play/ tonight, tonight/ I only believe in tonight / so for once/ throw your cares and travel with me/ travel with me/ travel with me/ travel with me/ I for one/ have long gone/ out the door and far away/ down south/ mouth to mouth/ to exhume a brighter day/ live for this/ chance at bliss/ this kiss that wants to form/ on the air/ everywhere/ as the fungus sun beats down/ on the nervous under-town/ planes are the shoes of clowns/ yeah yeah yeah /

X

THE POSTMODERN ID

I'm thinking about the old days,
how the hippies are not ageless as the sun rays,
I'm thinking about the ideals of 60's,
and though I don't believe in pixies

the effect of global warming on the unicorn
succeeded Piper At The Gates of Dawn,
the summer rain falls with as many hands,
as there are names for new rock bands...

I'm thinking about the imminent future,
there has to be a place still for Nature,
thinking about the state of poetry,
the young light has dawned on me...

the effect of global warming on the unicorn
succeeded Piper At The Gates of Dawn,
the summer rain falls with as many hands,
as there are names for new rock bands.

I'm trying just to think about the present,
and how my life could be so pleasant,
don't want to be distracted in daydreams,
by a woman as lovely as the sunbeams...

the effect of global warming on the unicorn
succeeded Piper At The Gates of Dawn,
the summer rain falls with as many hands,
as there are names for new rock bands.

I'm thinking about the doors of perception,
how literature is beautiful deception,
you might find the bedroom is hidden,
you might find the dawn is unbidden...

the effect of global warming on the unicorn
succeeded Piper At The Gates of Dawn,
the summer rain falls with as many hands,
as there are names for new rock bands
so try to pass the gravy over
Facebook now and be free.

Don't know what a Dorian Mode is,
but I know who Toad of Toad Hall is,
and the lady in my life is all missing,
and the music's only meant for kissing.

XI

DOWN IN THE PATCH WORK QUILT BELOW

I like the light and the flight of arrows
I also love the sound of running water
Down in the patch-work quilt below
Where the river of sadness used to flow

It's easy to trip up on a daisy
Lazy of us to let it get this way
Down in the patch-work quilt below
Where mad children splash and play

Art gets to its feet like a cartoon Bambi
She might go veggie for reasons of Disney
Down in the patchwork quilt below
Where the ego-loss breeze can freely blow

Heading down to the sea can free you
No-one knows how to free you but meyou
Down in the patch-work quilt below
Where we'll inevitably have to flow

XII

'GARDEN' IS THE PASSWORD TO MY IMAGINARY WORLD

Because it is recorded and online while this book is in the process of being written I will represent this instrumental. I had the idea – once a portion of my songs were recorded – to make an album of instrumentals – no words - all about my boyhood mythos of tunnels inside the oldest fell lined with free beer dispensers and fruit machines. In said mythos, you whisper the password 'garden' to the portal at the back of the cave on the face of the foothill Sea Ness (originally Seer Ness after a seer and his trance) to open it up and then can enter the tunnels. Because there are no words, the names of the songs would have to tell the story on this album, which saw us travel to the old USSR and make it home safely for dawn. Unfortunately it never worked out and I can't remember why but this instrumental is something that remains from the album, maybe the only thing.

XIII

WALKING THE BEAT

(impromptu spoken word piece)

Women can be very beautiful
they can be sharp-elbowed too
they think when we discern their beauty
we are being blinded by love
love is a banana custard to them
man's highest emotion to me
but single is my jingle these days
I sleep on a single mattress
if I ever do sleep that is
the dog'll be beside me
he's a symbol of gravity
and humour and katabasis
it's been a while since I've been in love
and what lovely dresses they can wear in summer
ones with floral patterns on
that come all undone -
it's winter right now
winter has her compensations
I'm sitting in a coffee-cake dining room
there's a Christmas tree
adorned with baubles and bright white lights
I suppose they should come down
it's the 2nd of January
Bertrand Russell's History of
Western Philosophy is on the table
some chocolate from Finland
some baccy some papers
some of my mother's driftwood art
Quality Streets which my dad
used to call Quantity Streets
and what else I don't know
a toothbrush that hasn't been opened yet

'THE ALARM CLOCK' BY JOHN F B TUCKER

John Tucker

I

THE DARK CARNIVAL DANCE

['The Dark Carnival Dance' has no words. It was an old favourite among my Cambridge friends and Cambridge band The Flood which I brought back from Warwick University, and when I went back to see The Flood in the holidays, I would try and teach them it. It's actually quite difficult to play. It has quite a few chords in it and I confess I did not write the first two chords, but heard someone else (Tom) at Warwick play them on the bass, whereupon I picked up the ball and ran with it, wrote the rest of the number, in terms of both rhythm and lead. So I thought I would still leave a trace of the instrumental in this instance in the lyric book. Somewhere there still exists a rudimentary version recorded through The Flood's binaural earphones!]

Soundcloud Rain

II

A POINT FIVE

[impromptu spoken word piece]

"I was going to pack it with content… a clock is only as fast as a cheetah - I said that at seven, seven. I got to the end and realised I hadn't pressed the right buttons on Ableton. You have to press the right buttons in life. That's more like it. Previously on this program oceans smile with liquid eyes and fill themselves with rain. Also I. T. might stand for Instant Travel too. Lucy in the soul with demons might happen to be an actual substance. And if a flower-press ending on cannabis could = a dialysis a love poem hoping to impress Flora could = more a motor. That was it. Then I realised – see I was trying to put Jimi's amp guitar on the vocal and it was full of feedback, squealing like an electric donkey then I realised the vocal hadn't gone down at all. I'd pressed the wrong buttons. I am hoping I pressed the right buttons this time. You have to press the right buttons. And now we're going to have a typing solo. I'm noticing the space bar is like the snare drum. I type with 2 middle fingers you know, like William Carlos Williams did."

John Tucker

III

TEST MONKEY IN B

We're aliens looking for life on Mars
aliens trying to make life in jars
aliens homesick for the stars
trying to find home in the all-night bars
in a world with no more la di da's
the sunset silts its knickers and bras
the night is bright with white guitars
the fat cats smoke their fat cigars
the wall inside is still the Tsar's
I watch the passing of the cars
I'm through with reading inveterate scars
in a room resounding with loud hurrahs

IV

SKUNKFOOT

(spoken word narrative to go over a drone of E)

Portability still seems the Apotheosis of Form: sometimes I can be walking along on a sunny day when I jump from the jungle to the Arctic to the Sahara. Mutation in consciousness itself, truth too simple to understand, these are gesture-without-motion-bones, like sadness gene and dreaming gland. It's not impossible to write an anti-poem. Love is not a mechanistic set of rules. Love was once aligned with madness, fever and intoxication. Love became grouped with language not God. Love became a tough word-combination. Love has no ego as everyone knows, and so it goes and so it grows. I for one think Lucy in the soul with demons may happen to be an actual substance. Travelling south, as I read Rimbaud, a rainbow smashed a railway train window. A baby cannot trip without memories... I remember "every atom ate our eyes." Our eyes: they are ingrown in the ocean's bellyful of wine, down in the seabed-orchard. There is angelic music inborn in the inner ear; but those whom the Gods wish to drive mad are sent the end of 'Bike' in their heads and madness is not something to be Romanticised as a return to Purity. Impunity seems more what the poet wants. He likes to float on the artifice of organic emotions through synthetic sounds, and is into exploring alternative histories suppressed by the overarching meta-narrative. For plastic surgery of the soul there are libraries. Poetry is the bike riding itself. Monopoly money will get us well, Monopoly money will get us bread, she picks the blue tac off the wall and says "my T-shirt is red". I put my wounds up on bright flags; I take the angel up the arse. To plug my senses in the mains might engage [!00 %] of my brains. It's all about a permanent reactivation of the Glastonbury Festival spirit. John Tucker is taking acid again. Money shags in the dark. Thoughts of one's greatness only diminish one's greatness. Skunkfoot is putrid demons excreted through stone. Love an army of fire. Fire needs some incentive to rise up. Shall I touch my heart with a red Bic biro? When all the air in outer space is consumed... The bird in the wood, it was definitely a horse, with solar spike I can use the Force, with R2D2 I cleanse my doors, I'm just trying to win my Star Wars. I'm starting to think in five musical parts at once. The Anon Throwaway as a new form could become an alternative currency to rival with money for the role of the real. Formal education is not for everyone. The yellow DogMuckels M atop the pole in the industrial park is the postmodern churchspire in the spiritual vacuum. Postmodernism is theme dissolved into message. Giant killers are frozen peas in the microwave. I look into the mirror though I shouldn't pool my sources. I'm not going to die at the age of twenty seven, watch the dreamtapes on repeat from a golden seat in Heaven. The heart beats to the rhythm of one. A fiver is surely cheese and onion flavour. Cataclysm is catalyst for the old cat that sat on the map of sound, just because the world is very round. If there were paper under my heart there would be writing on it and it would be art. I might ding it in compressed Space Age seconds.

(2002 - 2003)

V

THE WISH OF NIGHT

Madness swirls deep in the heart
A butterfly resides in you
A tragedy of feelings lost
surrenders to the wish of night

& in this world I can't explain
I know exactly where I am
Inside a crevice of desire
In the dreamy air of a lover's scent

Wherever you take me, that's where I'll be
In the weeping skies my mind gives up
& falls into the arms of sleep
I'd fade to know I thought of you

& the world has risen to my hands
& the earth murmurs beneath my feet
& the light of all that's good is true
if believing is the dawn of dreams

I guess that I'm afraid to tread
The purple skies for the risk of a word
But at least I'm sure of fear
As she gives me the strength to feel afraid

A whisper fathomed deep in mine
Well I don't even care to cry
& I don't care to face the edge
& plunge into the oceans dead

& the flame of love has lit my candle
& the sky has echoed my desire
& all the air is drawn into my lungs
& I know the secrets of the shade

& I know the wars that come from peace
& I know the mystery of love
& I know the resilience of the soul
& I'm sure that knowing you is true...

VI

FIZZY POP

I'm a clown, I'm a clown,
a clown in the circus of death.
I had a mate who sent the words
"Liquid Crystal Meth"
into space, into space,
and I was underneath it,
shower down, shower down,
make me feel alright.

No-one knows, no-one knows
what I went through in life.
The sadness shows, the sadness shows,
the trouble and the strife,
but under the stars, under the stars
I dream of love eternal,
shower down, shower down,
make me feel alright.

Fizzy pop, fizzy pop,
gets drunk in Monopoly Jail,
time goes slow, ever so slow,
as slow as a garden snail,
but ecstasy is a teddy bear
back in the garden of Eden,
I don't mind, I don't mind,
if you let me off my chains.

VII

INSTANT TRAVEL

Not far away in Magic Faraway Land,
there's poetry written on the bank notes,
sadness gene is smitten with dreaming gland,
the God Particle foreseen in the dust motes...

I. T. might stand for Instant Travel too,
NHS for Lucy in the soul with demons,
H20 stands for your hypothalamus tattoo,
ESA for Extra Sensory Allowance -

so how about we take a long holiday there?
You buy yourself a ticket with the opposite of bling.
You'll see through the frame of angel hair,
and might just need a love-song to sing.

Yeah yeah yeah, our love is the answer,
spinning in a circle around the tired sun,
waiting for the cure or vaccine for cancer,
seeming to be dreaming of the mid-day moon...

VIII

POETRY BUTTONS

Smart guitars between the stars
allow the ladies burn their bras
I don't ask for whom the beck
puts a necklace on her neck
let us have a go then, you and I
when we are tired of getting high
piss on the dawn when dad is dead
poetry buttons are in my head

poetry buttons for endless revisions
and helpless self-derisions
got to keep the quavers at bay
got to make the monster go away
the monster is not me
he lives beneath the deep blue sea

when all the air in outer space
is consumed without a trace
through a prodigious systematised
detuning of the strings we rise
would you compare me to a tramp
now my face is on a stamp
the poet makes himself a tea
now he's a mystic visionary

poetry buttons for endless revisions
and helpless self-derisions
got to keep the quavers at bay
got to make the monster go away
the monster is not me
he lives beneath the deep blue sea

voices voices everywhere
and yet not a drop to think
think of England when you're on
drink of physical hyperlink
all the world is on a page
where we spend our petty wage
engage with the dark night of the soul
that dreams in meaning like a troll

poetry buttons for endless revisions
and helpless self-derisions
got to keep the quavers at bay
got to make the monster go away
the monster is not me
he lives beneath the deep blue sea

John Tucker

IX

MONSTER OF ENERGY

'Monster of Energy' has no words! It sounds like The Velvet Underground jamming over a processed beat. When last I listened to it on Soundcloud, I got to the end and an advert flashed up, saying "originality is over-rated." I felt offended, questioned why I was still messing around with pop music as my father would put it, when I should be trying my hand at science. I turned the advert off before I finished listening to it, and focussed my energy on that vapid fashion statement suitable only for the rebellion of youth, pop music, if only to be free.

X

TEACHER OF MY HEART

I have found you you're the Teacher
of my Heart there's only one one
and though my mind is endless old
my tender heart is foolish young
and my timeless impassion'd battles
of emotion have sooooon begun.

You have lost me in a Teachers
whisky bottle drinking down down
down the shipwreck IS the treasure
harboured in my pirate undertown
where visions of the real Unknown
await us there when we drown.

They have told me it's a T-shirt
that's the body worn by the soul
O to have to discorporate and wash
our eyes in the Fairy Liquid bowl
it's good for you to know a goal
there is no music from a black hole.

John Tucker

XI

THE STAIRCASE

Once upon a time I was spiked
and thought I could fly
jumped right out of a window
and fell through the sky
somehow managed to land
on my smelly size 12 feet
seven stories below on
the heaving city street

now I tour the public schools
giving talks to forewarn
all the youths about drugs
in the world where they're born
taking LSD can change
your innate personality
take it from me please never
take the drug they call LSD

Splinter was the master of
the Turtles in the kids cartoon
and now he's dead and he's gone
beneath the morning moon
and I'm so sad to hear of that
for loss is painful in the heart
so may we all remember
him in our chosen art

Sitting at the back was a
boy whom I instantly knew
would do everything which
I had pleaded with him not to do
puffing on a cigarette
making all the others laugh
maybe he'll grow up to be
a kind of talking giraffe

When I fell I broke both legs
and did some damage to my spine
but I can walk if only slowly
and am in my headspace fine
I can still sing but not dance
which I never did much anyway
and I sing about health over
wealth at the dawn of this day

XII

WHISPER

(originally by Black Hole Myths when we were still called Funnelspirals)

I wanted to hear musac from a black
hole by Judas Priest but the guys
sent a parrot after a carrot and
through the conch to outer space
singing 'I won't always be an orange
just because you've sectioned me,
no I won't always be on Orange
just because you've sectioned me
but at any given time I'm working
in a crane' and Jesus said 'Syd by Ray
in a way Spiderman's handwriting
has been too obscene, I rake the
blade over the wishbone of my
legs Breakfast All Day/ gay
teachers can still lay eggs and
I won't always be a lemon just
because you've sectioned me,
no I won't always be on Lennon
just because you've session'd me
but at any given time Oedipus
is spying me up in the shower,
why I'll break the speed of speed,
rendered squander never priceless,
I'll never speed againe, at any given
time I'm a rare aquatic insect.'

(Hackney)

John Tucker

WORK WITH GRANT ASPINALL

Soundcloud Rain

APOLOGIA

Well, Grant Aspinall and I began recording together many years ago after my degree. At first he was mostly an excellent painter and extraordinary drummer who had but a few songs and poems and I was more a poet and guitarist, but now he does everything I do and more. He says you don't have to be Syd Barrett to do it, anyone can; and he also says it doesn't matter what age you are unless you are in a boyband! He really is such a cool and talented guy it is an honour to work with him. There was a time we released an EP called 'The A and E. P' under the name Funnelspirals on Soundcloud. It's still up there though by now we would probably take it down if we had the technological know-how on account of reading out of other people's books for spoken word parts. Also we have changed name to Black Hole Myths recently which was Grant's idea although it was me that already had not one not two but three songs concerning "music from a black hole." The point I'd like to make is that when you're in a two-piece you have to learn to share. Grant and I have made many, many recordings together in a secret location in Disneyland, Paris and there are some gems among them. To divide it all up and know what is mine and what not is not always easy – at least in terms of knowing what to put in your book of songs. There was a time when there was an album called 'Interstellar Artois' on my Soundcloud page and one called 'Eternal Full Moon' on Grant's Bandcamp page but that time is no more – I was told by sadistic voices to take everything I could down and in a moment of madness did and it made room for my solo work on Soundcloud but a few precious things were lost including a song which I wrote with a rhythm change and in a detuning which I considered my best work. We still have enough to get together a beautiful, singular Black Hole Myths album for Bandcamp in time. When it comes to my own book of songs, I would say if I did the music and Grant did the lyrics there's no way I can put that piece in my book. Likewise if Grant did the music and wrote the lyrics and I merely narrated the words like a spoken word piece, I wouldn't have anything to put in my book in terms of that number. What I am going to show then is stuff I can show you, stuff I had a hand in which is presently online, which therefore comes from the Funnelspirals E. P, or from another E. P. called 'Eternal Full Moon,' or from Grant's retrospective album 'Self Portrait # 357.'

John Tucker

I

COMING UP

(from 'The A and E. P.' by Funnelspirals on Soundcloud)

The face of stars he had no nose,
Einstein's prose equals Einstein's prose,
backward f, forward f, equals running through,
Frozen in red by Sensation in blue.

Fire sticks and alcoholics,
sonic sex and bright northern becks,
the face of stars he had no nose,
Einstein's prose equals Einstein's prose.

II

SNAKE SNAKE BUTTERFLY

(originally Oedipus Wrecks, now found on 'Self-Portrait # 357')

Snake snake butterfly,
lay me dead & close my eyes.
Angel serpentine, she
waits on the Other Side.
Give me your alibi;
give me chains to stop me fly;
give me night to soothe my blinded eyes:
so I can see the secrets of the skies.
We must rise, freedom
falling from our eyes,
unlock doors, it's a
perfect time to die, and it's
okay for baby we'll go insane
but don't reach out
too far for the flame.
Snake snake butterfly,
lead me to the Other Side.
Angel serpentine, she
waits on the Other Side.

III

INTERSTELLAR ARTOIS

This was originally called Musac From A Black Hole, and is an instrumental I wrote in London that made its way to 'The A and E. P.' by Funnelspirals before we changed name to Black Hole Myths. It's kind of dark and frightening and contains some excellent drums and guitar work too.

IV

THE BLAKE SONG

Only putting in things whose writing I have had a hand in, I have to put in this collaboration. It was Grant's idea to put Blake to music and he sent me home to think about it where I put together a guitar part and The Laughing Song by Blake which just seemed to go together. I went round Grant's the next day to record it and Grant was invited to sing and show us his voice as if for the first time. I was more into sprechstimme for this one – a German word meaning 'speaksing' – but Grant came out with some lovely contrapuntal and harmonious backing vocals over the guitar part. A fine piece of work, and maybe our best already, it wasn't long before Grant set it up that I read some critical prose about Blake from a book as a preamble to the music, which he affixed beforehand over some sounds he put together. A fine piece of work all round, it is found in its full form on 'The A and E. P.' by Funnelspirals and in its short form on 'Self-Portrait # 357' by Grant Aspinall. Maybe on looking back we shouldn't have put it online. It's the type of chord progression that you might imagine round Robin Hood's campfire.

John Tucker

V

SECLUSION

This is a piano piece found on Grant Aspinall's 'Self-Portrait # 357' – a retrospective he did. The piano piece was written by me as notes to Blake's Lamb then Grant hearing it urged me to put really long, gravid pauses in-between the chords, without changing a note, and changed the name to 'Seclusion' which is just right for the sound – for anyone who has been in the sterile surfaced hotel with locks on the doors that is hospital will know of these gravid pauses in this song and how slowly it seems to be going. So this is but an instrumental, that I would say was a collaboration in terms of me doing the notes and Grant doing the spaces between the notes!

Soundcloud Rain

VI

HOPE

(part of a spoken word piece by Black Hole Myths, found on the E. P. 'Eternal Full Moon' on
Bandcamp)

As I lie around careless of a map of sound
I love the lie of the land
where quiet gilly flowers
curtsey like ballerinas.
Streaming is vision.
Bees pollinate the garden,
birds pepper the lawn
where you let your flowery
blouse come all undone,
and a ray of light
soaks us all around.
The sky is a blouse of blue
hanging on the line.
Harmony thrums and
the sentient air is everywhere.
I lie back without a care,
sunlight blowing my hair about,
without a grey shade of doubt,
and deem it lazy of us
to let it get this way,
a day of careless play,
a carelessly radiant day,
all my troubles float away.

John Tucker

SOLO WORK RECORDED BUT NOT USED

BROKEN PART ONE

I had an idea for an album in which I would just sit, myself and an acoustic and a broken mic and play broken riffs, parts, fragments, like a kind of Deconstruction applied to music. I think I made eight or nine parts, each one called 'Broken' Part whatever it was and which were about fifteen minutes twenty minutes long each, with myself talking inbetween riffs ad-libbing, making things up. Here I have kept only the first part which is presented as a radio show and seems like the album The Madcap Laughs by Syd Barrett exacerbated to the nth degree like a narrative of madness. So this is how it goes, just myself and an acoustic!

John Tucker

THAT'S WHAT YOU GET WHEN YOU OPEN YOUR MOUTH

When the noxious toxins fade away
what's left of the day is probably good
is probably you the self that's true
the real feelings which the poet should translate

I spoke against September 11th in
the year 2000 but I soon forgot
because of the drugs we always took
and now I don't think I'll forget again

Such helpless fecundity of prescience
went across the board (there were other things)
for I spotted the pattern before it formed
and the CIA have now suggested why

If your dad is an international art smuggler
nicknamed Blue it can become
a new sense through which you can read
of future events as I did many times

They were testing times the days of my youth
and I can't see myself taking E again
and to look back makes me nostalgic now
makes me wistful for a day that has flown

The scene was a happening for a while
and I was a light, was a go-to man,
but for all that I've done and all I've said
I was still diagnosed and that will last for life

I'd say that to be on the crest of the wave
was very Heaven then and for a time
and I harnessed waves that have passed
through the Beat poets themselves in time before

It's a battle now just to write the words
but back in the day they used to say
I was good at them, I was good at them,
and I think I improved when it became too late

Of all the lines I came out with back then
I still kind of like the Rimbaudian idea
that oceans smile with liquid eyes
and fill themselves with rain

But that one is probably just to give voice to
an ancient silence I have found

Soundcloud Rain

and now the ground is rushing up
to meet me as I hurtle towards middle age

Sometimes your ordinary speech is
surreal enough to qualify as verse and
sometimes your verse pertains to
nothing but the condition of ordinary speech.

Some have said that I am the lion
from the heart of Poem Records and
that my name has been tattooed on
Track Five of Piper At The Gates of Dawn

John Tucker

WICKER CHAIR

(which started as a variation on a theme by Mark Velarde)

Baby I can see the tree kneel down
in Nick Drake's detunings before you
maybe it's just the purple germs accrued
on the windowpane maybe it's true
love what's love halved in chaos
love's the answer love victorious
love's the hope the heart literally needs
in order to survive without which
it can stop and I love to be alive
so I thank you for bringing us together
everyone loves you between us is the weather
on this fair day stay a while and play
troubles gone away love's the only way

CATHEDRAL CITY MINOR

I want to play in Cathedral City minor
because I can think of nothing finer
and cheddar cheese is one big celebration
that underwrites the name of a nation

well it's better than autistic silence
which itself is better than all modes of violence
and though I no longer watch telly
I might do if it just became smelly

bananas and nuts and Paracetamol
are not too pernicious for the mortal soul
like sleeping policemen there are others
when times were hard I remembered their brothers

but now sad things are not so funny
I'm waiting for the weather to be sunny
and maybe Soundcloud is raining
and the river is meant for training

O imaginary plectrum up in the sky
I hope you can play us a sweet lullaby
if I planted a tiny mic inside my chest
then I guess that it would attest to West

and Ableton Live is a new instrument
and I'd rather relate than I would invent
and I was the one that found the magic stains
and I never plugged my senses in the mains

John Tucker

OWL PERCHED ON A MIDNIGHT BRANCH

Owl perched on a midnight-branch O don't you even know
the branch is going to fall away with nothing down below?

I only heard your song last night, streaming through the air…
and now at night I sing to you with Revolution in my care…

it purifies the heart to think so I'm going to think a bit more.
It's a dream of elephant bones and I'm alone trying not to score.

I'm all alone with the stones and my dream went up a tree.
Ecstasia so much to answer for - the opposite of gravity.

If the windows were all washed – I mean every single one
you'd see nothing through them except the same old kitchen.

My very eloquent mother jams strawberries under Night
and I've a dream where it might seem the night-time is white.

When all the air in outer space is at long last consumed
then it's the same old story any treasure chest can be exhumed.

DARK DREAM RADIO AND THE INFINITE BROADCAST

(a spoken word piece)

I remember listening to my cheap cereal snap, crackle and pop in monopoly jail. Monopoly jail is what I call mental hospital. It's where you go for talking in Mumbo Jumbo Jet. Or hearing quavers, onjects, syllabubbles and sonic machinations at the threshold of sound. I don't think there should be an increase in hearing voices because I know their pain. I was once in a band called Secret Chord H. They were the 3rd of my five bands, the five bands I have been in. Secret Chord H was supposed to be a metaphor, a metaphor for some experiential pleasure that lies unknown and beyond but it ended badly when I was expelled for substances. Back then I had never heard a voice. I had heard of hearing voices but couldn't imagine it. Now there have been days where I have received literally hundreds of incoming e-mails. To be stranded by random access co-imagination is not a good thing. I think my friend and brother-poet Simon Pomery aka Blood Music likes the ideal of secret chord H and can separate it from drug-taking, which I never could. Anyhow, I don't think there should be an increase in voices. I think they make poetry quite artificial with their onslaught, their automated conveyor belt of poesis flowing room to room. Sirens on the rocks, that's the Ancient Greek myth, which most comes to mind. The notion of a tele-book is afloat. The omnijective interface of random access co-imagination is the new synchronised word. Through the room people come and go Smart-talking in magic alphabet radio. Weak, Wikileak tea could be writing done by voices. I might be the one to destigmatise hearing voices. Maybe they'll get looked back on as difference rather than illness. The dog sometimes barks at my so-called auditory hallucinations. It's a fine line between musical achievement and madness. I would like to play this all back and write this down. I prefer peace to hearing voices. I prefer the seagulls and their call.

John Tucker

JAMALADE X

From the ashes of the past
a new dawn rises now
a flower to the sun
who wears a pair of shades

from the dark night of the soul
a dawn has come again
the birdsong in the field
the day has just begun

losing my new look CV
I didn't get the job
but sounded out the bliss
of drifting free at last

from the loss there is some gain
from the night filled with pain
grumbling voices only come
when I turn to the book

when I turn to the song
I am free once again
the voices go away
like Night has done once more

inky tides they do recede
the coral of the trees it sways
and one thing I know for sure
that the new light is a door

through it I can find a way
to celebrate the transient day
love to be here and now
where the action always is

breakfast may be on the cards
the sound of sunrise is a joy
the rain of night has gone away
leaving clarity again

and I'd say the present tense
has been rinsed by a flame
sharpened by a fire here
cleansed of all its detritus

I'm alive and live for love
love to live and like my life
lend my ear to the sea

Soundcloud Rain

where the tune is afloat

stars have faded just for now
the motley morning now resolves
find my heart and know it's true
a first and final draft will do

there are no butterflies just yet
but Jokeo loves Ruliette
and the words can flow like wine
when the dark night is gone

although I now sing of dawn
I know the night will return
darkness holds the brightest light
sentient spark within its womb

but for now the day is born
and aloft on dreams I float
make it up as I go along
it's the nature of the song

beauty lives beside the fell
not that I have not known Hell
just that pulse is pulsing once again
farewell to the vampire, man

it was raining through the night
but now it seems alright
there's a woman on my mind
and she's lovely, wise and kind

who could know the secrets of the sky?
maybe we will never die
it doesn't seem such a bad lie
better than a hopeless sigh

one more door to walk through
soon the sky will be blue
spring will come and renew
all the amazing things you do

buttons pressed will not send
the pirate prince around the bend
enough to say I have this time
I'm the forefather of grime

another run but not to hide
who will be my cosmic bride?
enough respect to you all
sometimes still think of Paul

Eternity is always now
up the road is the Brown Cow
park the light inside your heart
this place is redeemable by art

98

MISCELLANEOUS SONGS AS YET TO BE RECORDED OR PUT ON AN ALBUM

John Tucker

ALAS THE DAY

Alas the daaaaaaaaay doesn't matter anyway
for there is a Night and heartbeats are bold
and hold me tight and Night is blessed
and filled with questions can not guess what
will happen next O maybe death
O electric street I'm feeling New Beat
there's silent fruit of sensory atrophy
growing on the vine like timeless wine
and later I might find my favourite line
take out your eyes and see in all directions at once
the infinite cocks are fucking the infinite cunts
I don't want my mum to ever fucking die
or join the silly gang up in the deep blue sky

Soundcloud Rain

BINAURAL EARPHONE MEDLEY

(some lesser known numbers by The Flood, some of which may have been recorded through binaural earphones but not used on their album)

Mumrah Greenback Skeletor Shredder Texas Pete Mr. Burns Deceptecons Vader Vader they were all there they were all there // you're playing you're messing you're fucking w/ the real // away away away away in farthest Spain, log on your brain, execute the plane // free the sparrows from the hedgerows nests and cages dissipating off to Africa calm equator sleep in frozen rock wake in sunburn I am the wind-cry robed in shadow // drug me sideways, drug me sideways, drug me north and south, drug me east and west, drug me all around, drug me sideways, // space is big and the edge is the middle and the middle is the edge and John is gone and he left his pink pyjamas on // apple juice apple juice and sweet little pretty pink things apple juice apple juice and sweet little pretty pink things.

John Tucker

BUTTERFLY QUEEN

[actually I seem to remember this one was recorded on the earphones way back in 2001]

Butterfly Queen so soon you'll die,
and soon you'll be needing all of your life,
so flyyyyyyyyyyyyyyyyyyyyyyyyyyyyyy,
so flyyyyyyyyyyyyyyyyyyyyyyyyyyyyy,
the beautiful garden where you reign,
butterfly's only queen for a day,
left the cocoon and dawned into light,
we don't know where we'll rest tonight,
where we'll get undressed tonight,
the school made rule book rules the day,
but school day's over time to play.

CHERUB

You are my brother's son
so you're cool whatever you do
quick to dance and quick to run
quick to smile with your eyes of blue
I will be sad without you here
but you'll be back I do not fear
and by then you will have grown
and you'll never walk alone

and the women will one day have to queue
to try and get a piece of you
you're a cherub just like your dad
and every time you leave I'm sad

you are such a natural boy
you are playing with your favourite toy
one more in the family
is a lovely thing to see
one day you'll drink some wine
and maybe later read some Quine
by then Dudu your teddy bear
won't be taken everywhere

and the women will one day have to queue
to try and get a piece of you
you're a cherub just like your dad
and every time you leave I'm sad

give your mother an easy time
she deserves it all to chime
love her true and honour your dad
always remember that drugs are bad
take each obstacle as it comes
learn to to do the right sums
I would say you could be a star
you might even learn guitar

and the women will one day have to queue
to try and get a piece of you
you're a cherub just like your dad
and every time you leave I'm sad

John Tucker

CREATE THE DAWN

Baaaaaaaaaaaaaaaaaaby we create the dawn
behind a veil where silence is born
and dawn conspires with the sea
and everything untrue recedes
and all that's left is you and me
and all that's left is you and me

No-one knows how to free you
no-one that is except for meyou
I was bitten by Lucozade snakes
but they're all gone up here in the Lakes
while I'm pursuing the redolent fume
of the mating queen into this room

Whom it seems is still in bed
whom it seems will give me head
I dress for Camden Town up here
for I don't have any baby fear
and when I get to the Promised Land
I'll make some friends and start a band

HAIRDRESS THE DAWN

Life is in bubbles flung out of the Tate
but knife is in trouble with lucky young Kate

burn and unlearn when she comes round
soon to discern blue sky is on sound

I sell yellow crayons to the invisible hand
I'd love to set foot in Gondwanaland

I too have explored the shapes of sadness
heartbreaking dawn on the verge of madness

a game is a wide, yellow circle with death
the centre so don't hold your breath

the circumference is closing in maybe forever
and life does not ask us to be too clever

it asks of us only to attend at the dawn
the dawn is a cordial cut up with brown

the very bone-marrow of beauty's to be
now and here and real and feeling free

you've got to escape the shape of the paper
it's planted with a lie tree in the centre

Man is an animal and man is words
and man is a word that is useless to birds

HOW TO BREAK THE LIGHT SPEED LAW OF NEUROPLASTICITY

You're The Juggernaut that's what you are
walk like an Egyptian and wriggle your little wing
like a winged chainsaw flying up in the cloud
swoop down and seal my soul and everything

For I'm the witness of this scene
I've read the pages of orange and green
I've got to keep my new yellow T-shirt clean
otherwise I'll offend the mating queen

On Grand-darth's Ship I went off a-sailing
suffice to say your horror-packet is served
and when I get back I think I'll give you a ring
for it's the least that you my demon have deserved

For I'm the witness of this scene
I've read the pages of orange and green
I've got to keep my new yellow T-shirt clean
otherwise I'll offend the mating queen

and when you score such a radical goal
it stays w/ you in your open, Holy soul
and you get no money and get no headlines too
but you've done what someone's just got to do

I KNEW THAT SHE LOVED ME

I escaped last night
into a heightened dream
from a dull and longing sleep

and the stars murmured
their cool ballad
to the approaching sky.

Secrets hung like ghosts
in the corner of my wanton world
all blurred and drugged too deep

and I knew that she loved me
from her invisible motions
and the dagger in her soft reply.

The questions concealed in her eye.

Her smile a luring prison.
Her blink a beautiful danger.
Her breath a poisonous magic.

And I knew that silence
would soon let slip its whisper,
knew that fantasy
had never been so real
and I knew that she loved me
because I knew everything.

I knew.

ICE CREAM VAN

(by Black Hole Myths)

Here comes the ice cream van
so get out your Ode to Death
vanilla flavour or bitumin #
and liquid crystal meth

Here comes the ice cream van
he'll give you a gun for a grand
and everyone queues up
to join his merry band

INWARD TO WANDER

Here comes a voice
I must be leaking
there is no choice
the song is in C
I travel quite far
all on my own
to Zanzibar
by xylophone
by xylophone

Most of my dreams
are a steaming midden
sometimes it seems
hyper-vision is close
I travel quite far
interrogate my soul
by bullet atop
a telegraph pole
a telegraph pole

Inside their storm
I drive a straight line
and try to keep warm
like coming up
I travel quite far
though I am vexed
by what might be called
predictive text
predictive text

Flashbacks flash back
a lightning bolt
is in a God Simulation
and daggering down
I travel quite far
and now becomes then
and know that the beck
is a fountain pen
a fountain pen

Never be still
or you'll get a parking ticket
I enter the cave-paintings
up on the wall
I travel quite far
carrying my toothbrush
travelling light

to the centre of night
to the centre of night

There are no customs
on the conscious/
unconscious border
no passport control
I travel quite far
smuggling Fruit Gums
right back to Rome
like Arthur Rimbaud
like Arthur Rimbaud

KILL

(Oedipus Wrecks)

My eyes sting,
my teeth are bleeding raw,
too much thought
to make me sick.

Stinky clothes
and mouth become
my skin and all these
fruits – I want to kill.

Give my hope,
surrender to the tide,
you can take
my remains but

I must go, to
wash the poison
from my eyes, before,
before, before I kill.

John Tucker

LE LITTLE LAPIN ON LE LAWN

Le little lapin on le lawn,
trembling in the dusky dawn,

forlorn as fallen autumn leaves
is the wave that misbehaves,

it makes you melancholy mad,
where the wave-forms terminate,

mind the gap where mirrors clap,
you don't need meaning on a plate,

you're dying slowly as the light
pours forth from the glowing east,

the sun a hedgehog in the air but
slow and Bible-black the beast,

O little lapin on le lawn,
who sheds a secret tear for us all,

sup the flowers like a cup
before the rusty autumn falls.

Soundcloud Rain

L. F. T.

Crash your party on LFT
it seems the brain is an open sea
crash your pirate ship into a monster
if you can still believe that you're free

when all the darkness
floods back through you
you've got to be true

there's little point in trying to pretend
we don't know where the story will end
I wish I was away with the cloud-change
I wish I was away with the mothership

crash your skiing trip into the roof
I love you I love you I need much small proof
crash your cigarette straight from the net
see Jokeo is in love with Ruliette

when Planet X just
comes back through you
you've got to be true

there's little point in trying to pretend
we don't know where the movie will end
I wish I was away with the fairies
I wish I was away with the star-beams

John Tucker

LOOK TO THE PEACHYVAN

(a song heard in dreams)

Look to the Peachyvan
every moment that you can,
to eating sweets on the back of the bus,
and playing Tetris too.

Look to the Peachyvan,
driven by the driver man,
carrying kids to school and back,
comfortable as an old shoe.

Look to the Peachyvan,
and have a new contingency plan,
it's done some miles, heard some song,
the kids say it's a banger.

Look to the Peachyvan,
drawing Alice closer to Pan,
long live the birds and the bees,
and don't end on a cliffhanger.

Look to the Peachyvan,
see the triumph if you can,
if the song seems it came in dreams,
it's probably because it did.

Look to the Peachyvan,
try and revert imagination's ban,
the effect of global warming on
the unicorn is a postmodern id.

LOVE ON SICKNESS BENEFITS

You'll bet I say this to all the fit girls
but I look at you and see only purple, silken swirls
I'd buy you troves of redolent flowers
the useless proof of a thousand hours

get out of my head, get into my bed, (baby)

To word/ hope/ dream you is not enough
you hit me w/ the pollen it has to be the real stuff
I'd sip from your eyes and taste your very name
like mother's home-made strawberry jam

get out of my head, get into my bed, [baby]

and we can chink pelvises like champagne flutes
atop the fell wearing leather walking boots
I see that your eyes are under-sea green
and dream I'm on some yellow submarine

get out of my head, get into my bed, [baby]

If love on sickness benefits can be done
it requires I imagine more imagination
and while I heard a poem is the opposite of bling
I don't need power just reasons to sing

get out of my head, get into my bed, [baby]

John Tucker

LOVE YOUR NEIGHBOUR

(recorded through state of the art binaural earphones in The Flood but not used on their album)

Love your neighbour till your girl gets home
I'm fleeing the town in my neighbour's clothes
love your neighbour in her underwear
I wonder what goes on under there

and you'd better repent
for all the money you spent
now you're dove has been sent

Love your neighbour when you're all alone
I left my message on your answerphone
love your neighbour with her tricks and lies
ask no questions hear no lies

and you'd better repent
for all the money you spent
now you're dove has been sent

Love your neighbour till the war is gone
I think they think that's not fair on John
love your neighbour when the war is over
treat your neighbour like your long lost lover

and you'd better repent
for all the money you spent
now you're dove has been sent

LOVERS AND FOOLS

Lovers and fools are breaking their own rules in The Game
mad children play unaware of an end to their game

sailors are losing the world and riding the breeze
angels and thieves are kissing at the tips of the trees

say is the waxen candle worthy of the flame?
You answer the doors when love calls you by the name

pirates and whores are opening the chambers of the sea
if you see the key please don't be afraid to be free

policemen and clowns are stuck in dull towns with the vain
saying hello and welcome to life my name is Pain

gypsies and tramps are keeping oil lamps in the dark
through city streets people beat electric and loose dogs bark

say is the waxen candle worthy of the flame?
You answer the doors when love calls you by the name.

MURDER IS DEAD

(Oedipus Wrecks)

Fuck this, fuck that, fuck me yeah,
I wish that I had been there,
been there to saaaaaave Jesus,
I'm sure he meant to please us.

Murder is dead,
murder is dead,
murder is dead.

We're young and filled with semen,
we're going to break some hymen,
we'll make the cops turn in their badges,
we're going over all the edges yeah.

Murder is dead,
murder is dead,
murder is dead.

Soundcloud Rain

ON THE YEAR DOT

The energy it takes to pick up the guitar -
I saw a flash of light like from a passing car -
then the dust it came, came parachuting down -
and wild packs of dogs were sniffing about the town -
a disparate bunch of things made a necklace there…

in the blank amnesia of Heaven did we wake
when fissile was the rock and dead the fairy cake?
Is the internet still working can it start a war?
Is the soul still sacrosanct as it was before?

A pulverised McDonalds is a pulverised Pizza Hut
and looking round the town both of them were shut.
As a random bystander I stood beside the lake
and heard the ashen forest of the radio break
and nothing came along through the intercom...

in the blank amnesia of Heaven did we fly
when soaring like a rocket through the unbroken sky?
Is the dream still freedom and do we still agree
that Freedom's Man's main, psychic thread in 2023?

I dreamed of a Paradise where gilly flowers dawned
but now walk in the dark of which the Ancient Ones warned…
stars slept in the open like around a Boyscout fire
and looked down on the dead land from their tree-ascending choir,
and saw the mess that Man had made of the world….

In the blank amnesia of Heaven did we wash
when we found that there was nothing left to do with dosh?
Can we erase the debt and free Assange and have Detente?
Do we even know exactly what it is we want?

The dog needs to go out into the garden for a wee,
he's pee'd on mum's speaker and the speaker isn't free.
The garden is an eco-toilet for most natural things
and fairly soon we'll see again the birds sing with their wings,
when spring gives hope as it always seems to do.

In the blank amnesia of Heaven did we swim
when love was like a drug and we went out on a limb?
Did the dawn still come and was poetry reborn?
Will there be no forgiveness if we do squander the dawn?

John Tucker

ONE

If you dabble with the alphabet
You swallow the frogspawn of O' Neil

If you follow sweetness-sweetness
You end up in the back of the real

If you fall asleep with Ulysses
You might dream of a new song

If you ever wake up againe alive
You'll see song is where you belong

If you ever get stuck on a verse
There's always tea and then the bat

If you deem this to be your quarter of
The pancake mix then that is that

If your dream's too full of imagery
You might need to wake up fast

If you're on strong medication now
Your demons could be a thing of the past

If we deem your dream book trite
We'll put some thought into it

If we rename the days of the week
We might go more slowly through it

If it's ten at only ten to seven
Then it's still getting to be eight

If we're still on the road to Heaven
Let's not be early, let's turn up late.

OPTIMUS PRIME'S HOMETIME

(by Black Hole Myths)

The chainsaw of my heart has come undone, / blanes is a liquid knife by Mars, / winners are allowed fucks instead of FACE, / transphiloquising adimals and stars. / Clocktick clock being clocked off by clocktick, / clocktick clock not being clocked off by Time, / The Universal Mind's moon meat man met, / and he said a little lamb being fed a bottle of milk is being chainsawed in the face by Optimus Prime. / Well the sun hanged himself from a length of daisy chain, / and it's too late to sheathe your liquid knife, / Barnes has scored a chicken in the wood, / and wingers are allowed bikes in the afterlife. / You can taaaaaaaaaaake a horse to water but / you can drink the horse, drink the horse / and did those feet in ancient times / raindown and walk the sun? Of course. / Raindown and walk the sun? Of course.

John Tucker

RENEW THE BLUE OF BEDE

Well I just want to say any word can be spelled in any way
and any guitar solo too played in any way, black or blue

all the boundaries have dissolved all the subjects become one
this could be so much fun underneath the moon

still I dream of a secret chord because I'm easily bored
and the switch is thrown like the dog with his bone

and I hope the universe is not really in a hearse
and the universe-hearse not in your soul-hole

and I don't need to renew the big black and big blue
for the dog's already down the one that has no brain

and this one's the best this one passes the test
even if that mild dream is but a bird with a scream

try any triangle twice from this angle it's nice
from the D to the E to the A then to the D

and full fathom five, full fathom five thy father lies
could never be any other number because

the old poet Virgil says "there are tears in things"
and so I still believe in the invisible kings.

SOLILOQUY

I felt a leaf
I fell out of life
Probably no-one else knew
But then there may be some

It was vexed was the edge
A playground swing
Swung empty of person
Ad infinitum

I looked around
At the new blue
On the other side
Like it were the same

I'd hurtled through colour
Evicted my teacher
And landed like Nietzsche
At the height of a dream

By this time
Some fan mail arrived
I'd developed an e-mail
Address back home

My password was whitecrow
And it was a word-chord
And for all my passwords
It was the same

I fly over oceans
As instant as gravity
Intending to transcend
The praise and the blame

Exploring the truth
Within Red Indian poetry
I liberate myself
On the big walrus drum

The walrus is Paul
Gone under Gondwanaland
Chasing the dragon
Right back to the womb

John Tucker

I mediate the tribe
And the spirit world
Halfway to Iceland
Where the dog's in his tomb

I've seen a bit too much
But it was just a holiday
And it always ends up
In a policy hot room

Henry the Hoover
Has become monarchy
In the happy world of Haribo
Or so it would seem

THE BLUE ROOM

Let's go and check, check out the room,
let's go and check, check out the room,
let's go and check, check out the room,
check out the blue, check out the blue,
let's go and see, see what we find,
wear an emotional condom before you fuck my mind,
see if the dagger stabbed in the table,
is beautifully dangerous or dangerously beautiful,
let's go and feel, feel John and Paul,
let's go and tell stories quite tall,
let's go and laugh the loudest of laughs,
let's go and feed the talking giraffes,
let's go and read the secret hieroglyphs,
let's go and smoke seven straight spliffs,
let's go and love, love all that we find,
wear an emotional condom before you fuck my mind.

John Tucker

THE DISSIPATED HOUSE

The man in a black suit
sat in the backroom
drawing on a fat one
until his house came undone
brick by brick it floated
out into blue ether
leaving only open
empty space beneath her
open to the weather
he couldn't tell whether
love had truly spoken
love had truly woken
or if it was a bad thing
like when it started raining
and all of his bricks were
floating in the atmosphere
trapped in channels too deep
tears too sad to weep
made their presence known
when he couldn't find his phone
it was ample in suspense
it was in a new tense
then it all came falling down
like the tears of a clown

THE HAPPIEST EVER TOM

(by Black Hole Myths)

Boom boom boom well this is not a room
bigger than a room we're going to have a drum
boom boom boom no this is not a dream
bigger than a dream we're going to have drum
going to have a drum going to have a drum

we're bounding in magic circles in space
we deem the face of stars to be off his face
we'll call it the moon and if we die soon
movements in the air will leave a sparkly trace
leave a sparkly trace leave a sparkly trace

glow in the dark stars upon the ceiling
do not preclude the translation of feeling
move to the music, that warm shaken air
whose meaning is nothing but faces in the fire
but faces in the fire but faces in the fire

John Tucker

THE INDIVISIBLE KING

(a psychtrance number written on returning from The Secret Garden Party)

Who do you think's the indivisible king?
His name is writ on a butterfly wing

A fireface moon and a frozen rock sun
Collide in a dream and the dyes start to run

But Hamlet's been healed by a shaman with spells
And vowels are our souls and words can be cells

You are who you love and not who you are
So set the controls for the prettiest star

The wings of a butterfly will bear my weight
One can be savage and one can be great

My temple is simple it's inside your brow
Each day is a new religion now

To sleep on the ceiling w/ feelings of love
Or sleep on the feeling w/ star-tracks above

Say is the wick worthy of the flame
And as play dies and becomes the Game

Is ecstasy mc squared or a dove
Is numbness to love just as painful as love

And while I'm uttering crushed butterflies
If you ask no questions you'll hear no lies

127

THE POEM POLICE

The Poem Police came through the bedroom wall,
said 'no gaseous music down the hall!'
My purple patch was decidedly blue,
I said 'we're not allowed to mix with you'.

Soon water went for a naked prance,
it was then that Legolas started to dance.
They'll cuff you up in the radio station,
put the microchip of peach into the open.

Noughts and crosses quelled by The Poem Police,
they said 'take off your snakeskin jacket please' -
I said 'I'm going to win the Snowbell Prize',
joking and smoking in their growing eyes.

Effort is inversely proportional to success
so the Poem Police cried and just said "YES!"
and we beat them on the head w/ a beastful flower
and introduced them to the transience of power.

John Tucker

THE SPEED OF DARKNESS

Loooooooooooooove, love, gooooooood for the brain:
the more you eat them the more you go insane.
Loooooooooooooove, love, gooooooooood for the heart:
the more you eat them the more you break apart.

They're dissipating energy with spiralling entropy,
they're falsifying visions with indoctrinated feelings,
they're colouring perception with vague mysticism and
you've been plugged in to the mental health system.

Loooooooooooooove, love, gooooooood for the brain:
the more you eat them the more you go insane.
Loooooooooooooove, love, gooooooood for the art:
the more you eat them then the miracle will start.

You've got to get sober from the green yellow M.
The street is a bird's nest high atop a ragged tree.
Her being isn't bound by her green yellow them
and the crows are the ones supposed to fix the TV.

With freedom comes energy with energy happiness
with happiness feeling well not just feeling crappiness.
The way she holds Nirvana, the extinction of consciousness,
in a goldfish blink in her eye is quite priceless forever.

THE TRIAL

(by Black Hole Myths)

It's typical to get stuck behind a tractor
when there's somewhere else you'd rather be
with someone nice that's a Strange Attractor
as they call them in Chaos Theory
then the smell of muck-spreading fills the air
as you're overtaking the slow coach

back down in town it's a cruel situation
it's a rush to be going nowhere fast
around about here they call me a seer
and my squalid squat is a thing of the past

I miss the city when I'm up in the Lakes
I miss the country when I'm down in the city too
I'm always nibbling on mother's fairy cakes
I'm happy moving on to something new
the grass is always strong on the Other Side
but it's not good for short term memory

even up here where the light is so clear
there's a dealer whose clues can enlighten
it's been said before and I don't wish to bore
but the heart of the sun can frighten

man I love the supple light in spring
I love the beck and the birds and flowers too
I cannot wait for compress sans everything
but I love dawn's hundred hues of blue
to meet the wheel and sing of synchronicity
and laugh at Flarf in the meanwhile

even the eel is learning to feel
and the lay of the land is a playground
come with your team into the hot dream
when the band have found their true sound

[Note: co-authored with my imaginary friend Matt]

John Tucker

UNDERNEATH THE APPLE TREE

Underneath the apple tree
before University
I sat down for a strum

light was falling in blank pages
and I waited there for ages
in a world where words won't come

Now I've gone back to the start
with a heavier heart
like an apple about to fall

It's a different world out here
where the Fear is never near
but I long for a call from Paul

I don't need a set of keys
there's a kiss in the breeze
and there's credit on Tap

dreams are seamless as it seems
but who would renew my dreams
as I wander without a map

soon enough I felt a leaf
and I fell out of life
probably no-one else knew

the shapes of sadness are round
like holes in a map of sound
that the weather gets in through

VITAL SIGNS

(Oedipus Wrecks)

Smile like a smile just to smile,
cast to heaven for a while...

let's rip holes in the boat,
throw the captain overboard,
throw the angels off the bridge,
death comes and stops me getting
bored of life's soul-machine.

What we need is energy,
show me all your vital signs,
what we steal is what we need,
what we need to feel alive,
for I'm alive with vital signs.

Back to Hell to plunder wings,
let the ritual now begin,

come and ride the waiting beast,
ride it gone into the fire,
ride it to the waiting feast,
my baby's waiting to get higher,
to get higher, to get higher...

what we need is energy,
show me all your vital signs,
what we steal is what we need,
what we need to feel alive,
for I'm alive with vital signs,
yeah feel alive with vital signs.

Come again there's much to do,
don't you know that I love you?

John Tucker

LOOKING TO THE FUTURE: A FEW POSSIBILITIES FOR FURTHER RECORDINGS

VISUAL RADIO IN MARY'S ROOM

I remember visual radio swirling all around,
the head of the seer so full of broken ground,
and how purple and digital it all really seemed,
like I'd taken Nirvana pills of which I'd dreamed,

now they've locked me out or I've sobered up,
I've got nothing to sup except my coffee cup,
seems like only water is the brand, new sense,
seems like only the present is the brave, new tense,

there was nowhere safe to rest my eyebeam
that didn't incur "sex" in the conscious dream,
you can call it hyper-vision if you really want,
when the switch is thrown and there's italicised font,

but to boring old water everything has returned,
and I can't quite tell if anything has been learned,
through the motley shoals of Technicolour fish,
she was with me there and that was always my wish.

John Tucker

ENLARGING THE SKY

One star leads to another star,
that's why we're enlarging the sky.
Christening another new guitar,
one more summer night goes by.

Travelling by predictive text,
you have no time to tend to your hair.
I don't know what'll happen next,
but I love to breathe the summer air.

For all the summer air is good,
that's why we're enlarging the sky.
Yes it is, the summer air is good,
that's why there is no need to sigh.

Glass trees are black when you're gloved in sleep,
drift past as you dream away,
don't go getting in too deep,
come back before the light of day.

For all the summer air is good,
that's why we're enlarging the sky.
Yes it is, the summer air is good,
that's why there is no need to sigh.

SPACE IS BIG

Space is big
space is big
space is big
space is big
space is big
space is big
space is big
space is big
and the edge
is the middle
and the middle
is the edge
is the middle
is the middle
is the edge
John is gone
John is gone
John is gone
John is gone
John is gone
John is gone
John is gone
John is gone
and he left
his pink pyjamas
pink pyjamas
pink pyjamas
and he left
his pink pyjamas
they were on
find a bridge
find a bridge
find a bridge
find a bridge
find a bridge
find a bridge
find a bridge
find a bridge
or we'll never
live forever
live forever
or we'll never
live forever
live forever

John Tucker

THE ALPHABET DOVE

The alphabet dove flew over the sea
I dreamed my love was in a car with me

one pint of beer does not go very far
she got out and went into a different car

my love, my love, you are not mine
I dreamed you were deadly as the sunshine

at night I gearshift to beer number four
without you here my life is a bore

I'll save it for when I am aged eighty
and the future is not what it used to be

I dreamed we drove into a far town
I think the sunlight was pouring down

my love, my love, when will we rise
I saw such freedom burn in your eyes

this position I hold is getting quite hard
it's use just once and then discard

FARTING OUT OF THE WRONG ORIFICE

The skull is not an orifice
unless you smoke too much cannabis

but as for those there are plenty
although not quite twenty

out of which we can fart
and we can call it art

especially out the mouth
living down in the south

I think the art begins with Joyce
which influenced my voice

before I read it, through my dad,
and then it became a fad

like recording through earphones
or building a house with sandstones

in the sky when possibilities
change in golden alchemies

and mud is gold under one's feet
and change is good and life is sweet

John Tucker

UP IN THE SKY

I heard about the mad, stifled witness,
taking a bullet for any old her,
he took a long flight over the ocean,
and had to change flight up in the air...

don't you know that's not technically possible -
a dog is a dog is a dog is a dog!
Maybe the gap between us is impassable
but I'd still upload my brain to your blog.

A bird now flies outside my window.
It must be guns that caused the dispute.
A waif in a safe is a bimbo in limbo
and a poet in Italy should wear a suit...

O don't you know our love could be beautiful -
a dream is a dream is a dream is a dream!
Maybe the gulf between us is impassable
but I'd still go with you to the extreme.

My dog has dementia, my dog is insane.
My dog has dementia, my dog is insane.
My dog has dementia, my dog is insane.
My dog has dementia, my dog is insane.

ABOUT THE AUTHOR

I can remember first coming to awareness, clicking on if you like. It was in a chalet in a resort called Brockwood Hall in Whicham Valley, Cumbria. I was sitting with my father and mother at a table eating breakfast. I found a plastic yellow submarine in the Cornflakes box. As far as I remember it there were two – a lucky box! My father's language was perceived as microphone static; but my mother I remember saying "you like 'Yellow Submarine' don't you John?" I said an enormous roadgoing YES and that was it - I was awake – and aware – and that was my coming to consciousness or rather earliest memory. I realised I had to start trying hard to understand what my father was talking about.

I don't really remember writing my first book at seven although by now I have since read it. At seven I wrote a book performing 4 functions: to predict the net and the cloud, to contain the first disclosure of the idea that a clock is only as fast as a cheetah, to conduct an experiment into the maths for the red and black skin cell (or something like that) and to separate the pollen I found from its name. It was a book with a heartbeat that made the sound of footsteps in the locked attic where it was kept.

Then, when my father sold his art dealing business at the fall of the Berlin Wall, I attested to the pestilence – it was a mistake! Any hope I was dreaming was extinguished when it happened a second time proving plastic can grow - and I shouldn't say any more than that. They were signs of the unpresentable kind, and no I would not say they were music, whom it seems was already my inspiration.

By the age of 12 I proved it was possible to change the colour of white skin through maths albeit only very slightly – it was maths I wrote at 7 and hadn't yet read. It was simply a case of constructing an algorithm that sublimates numbers and letters on the same cellular level. For example I started one poem with the line "I have a scar+ that is a red and black," employing a + sign for the 'F' of scar+. These are Syd Barrett's colours of Hell. I started to add to it, left it a case of adding up: when I got to the end of my exercise book I wrote on the front of it "2 John Tucker English E" and on the front of the next one "English John Tucker Harecroft 1." Still counting I wrote in my maths book:

"Colour circles red. How many circles?
Colour triangles blue. How many squares?
Colour oblongs orange. How many triangles?"

It was then that I wrote of being 4 years old and being on holiday in Sweden – when my dad bought me a new bike which I crashed into the nettles. For my entry on number 5 I used my brother Dr. Robert who was five years old. Six was a short story – very psychedelic – about drinking some lemonade and then shrinking and shrinking until I was six inches high and walking towards the chess board I had left lying around. The numerical ascent continued in that selfsame story where I had a big adventure and grew back to my normal size.

So it was when I reached the age of 11 or 12 that I was visibly marked by such early writings. It proved I was not just a passive slave as "witness" but an active part of it all. Around this time – I was coming top of English every term at the most expensive Prep School in the known universe – and I remember I wrote two long prose poems, one called The Fire and one called The Sea which were meant to go together and encrypted something specific I had in mind. By the age of 12, when Hannah was herself by now 7, we all got together and wrote and recorded

John Tucker

The Road to Heaven by Noj And The Mob. That was my first album and already a point in an arc that dated back to when I was seven.

It was then that I left Prep School and started drinking and smoking – and things became slightly more wrong-headed and self-destructive. By 16, I was in Oedipus Wrecks who gigged in London. My mnemonic for the strings was Even A Dick Gets Big Erections, my ideal genre Grime way ahead of its time, the coin on my tongue "amazeballs." We – two friends and I - attained the face of stars which was indeed amazeballs. Still, we had to walk away.

By 1998 we find I was in a third band – Secret Chord H – which was meant to be a metaphor for some experiential pleasure that lay unknown and beyond. We made it to the radio with a song called 'Dream with Open Eyes'. There was also a kind of B-side concerning an old cassette that had a small pause in the song where the reel was cut and resealed. The song about it just went "another, another, another fucking joint," so that was one experiment to see if the pause could be done away with. I also started a poetry mag at the same time and was writing anonymous love poetry.

In ordinary speech in the year 2000 I predicted the God Particle from looking at dust in a late ray of light angling in before the big machine was built in Switzerland. That year, 2000, I also spoke against September 11th to the day, prophesied the Plough's alignment with the landscape for the first black president of America, got the name and concept of my future University tutor-to-be's future paper bang on but as the ideal for the book I myself would write, and wrote the highest-marked English Literature A-level exam essay in the nation. The day my A-level results came through I went down south straight away to live with Paul in Cambridgeshire. We started a band, my fourth, called The Flood, after many things, including a quote from Rimbaud, and learned to detune the guitars, and only recorded through state-of-the-art, binaural earphones, belonging to another band member, which made us feel very cutting edge.

I went to Warwick University around 2002 and found my ideal for a book had that year just been published by my tutor. Meanwhile the first mobile phone I had used to reverberate the rhythm of 'William Tell' through every technological inlet in the room before it rang from home. I wrote some good pieces, some of which have now been turned into songs, and left with no degree, went back to Cambridge where I promised on the binaural earphone record I'd "plug my senses in the mains." I lived in the shed in the band's back garden then. We had fun. We were a Cambridge-based jam band that worked often in full de-tunings in the middle of the night and as I say only recorded through state-of-the-art, binaural earphones. There was an abandoned primary school down the road commandeered by the youth artists for a happening scene. The Flood were one in-house band and there were also poetry readings and art exhibitions put on. Apparently the songs we write when young are the songs we keep when old but the poems we write when young are not the poems we keep when old. Anyhow, two bands went to Europe in two cars and had more fun. The other band changed personnel and gained slick, processed beats and we came home and did up the house.

Getting kicked out the band for weird behaviour is what happened although I used to call it walking away from music to pursue poetry and get a degree this time of asking, which I did from Lancaster University. I was hospitalised during the degree and after that degree, I was diagnosed mentally ill. Around this time the Plough would hone in to alignment with the fell for Mr. Obama's election, a vision only possible at my family home in the Lakes. The Flood fell north to see it and we had a healthy time, the only healthy time we ever had. After that I went to London, witnessed the lootings, even lived rough on the streets for a while, saw some old

141

friends, busked, played a good gig at the Hospital Club. It seemed my name was tattooed on Piper At The Gates of Dawn. The pint glass exploding from thin air in the capital was beautiful.

When I came home to the north, well, I built the Tower out of magical books like one emanating fragrance and one with a vanished line; I cooked the tape in the AGA when its pause was done away with; I worked for years at a numinous purple-bleeding PC screen in an experiment into post-humanism; and when my father passed I was the one to discover the James P D Tucker sheet where pictures bloomed or even grew. The pictures seemed to depict the lyric to one of my old songs from Oedipus Wrecks but the sheet was not and is not my sheet. It was then that I wrote a poem that falsifies the Nirvana barcode and seems to be the one.

When I say it seems to be the one you have to remember that when I was 16 I had already come into contact with Rimbaud's colours of the vowels, Keats' Negative Capability, Gray's precursor to Romanticism in a graveyard, the Beats with their discussion of the last poet's last poem, the Merseyside Beats with Top of the Poets, the Central Nervous System of the earth in Ted Hughes, The Lords And The New Creatures by Jim Morrison, Blake's proverbs, the lyrics of Tricky, Thom Yorke, Nirvana, The Smashing Pumpkins – and more – and I was thinking about what my own contribution would be – and I remember sitting in a Glastonbury tent with a notebook open, stone, looking at a golden string on a guitar, whose mnemonic let's not forget was Even A Dick Gets Big Erections, writing about the guitar string and knowing my contribution would have to be more than that – and so I feel with this falsification of the Nirvana barcode I have found that thing I was looking for – a handle – a time-faring entity – maybe even a point.

By now I have had several books go out, some of them un-published afterwards. I've never really written about the nature of madness apart from in fits and spurts. My mother says: I was never that drastically insane and all I really needed was to be able to grow my hair and wear what I wanted and be myself but my father was so strict he physically forbade me from growing my hair. He – who was an original hippy in the 60's – wanted better outcomes for me, in terms of the English class system – than he got for himself. He thought I would work in television – I don't even watch TV anymore. He thought I would be a barrister – I no longer break the hollow claw but I used to every day. He thought I would be a writer – in that he was right, but I am yet to make any of the books he suggested - like exploring the origins of the Liverpool F. C. football songs in pubs and gutters, or like walking in a circle round the Lakes, or like the campus novel where a Muslim is being watched by the State and a breakthrough in nuclear fusion is suppressed for monetary reasons. No, the books I have brought out are not the ones he suggested and probably a lot less sensible too.

I came back from a holiday to Italy very recently thinking what is wrong with much of my page-bound poetry is that my mother has had a heart attack and finds it depressing and oppressive too whereas remaining in the realm of song doesn't incur that problem. A song like 'Kill' by Oedipus Wrecks – which I wrote at 15 or 16 – seems to have meaning and to have soared over the heads of the audience when I played it first time at a gig in Camden as well as representing a moment when I nearly came out as a full-blown rock star with antecedents in rock star literature. These days I am said to be nearer a beautiful mind than a rock star, with my mental illness. Getting back from the recent holiday in Italy I also managed to sort out the inchoate morass of my writings, recordings and photographs on my blog, and found that only the book of songs had any audience whatsoever and even then it was but one fan. To have but one fan is enough for me, to keep going, and so even at the age of 41, with no chance of getting a record deal, I will keep up this stance of being an alright guitarist, who sings a little bit, and hopes to be found among that rarefied number of writers whose song lyrics work as verse.

John Tucker

PHOTOGRAPH FOUR

INSERT PHOTO OF FLORA'S FACE STOLEN FROM FACEBOOK. UNLIKE THE
PREVIOUS THREE PHOTOGRAPHS THIS ONE IS NOT MINE I MEAN I HAVE NOT
TAKEN IT. I MEAN I HAVE NICKED IT BUT NOT TAKEN IT IF YOU KNOW WHAT I
MEAN. I MEAN CAN WE SHARE WHAT IS POSITED ON THE WEB? THIS PHOTO
CONTAINS ZERO SUGAR. IT MIGHT HAVE TO GO IN THE RECYCLING BIN. I MEAN
DREAMS IN THE RECYCLING BIN GO ROUND AND ROUND. THIS WOULD HAVE
BEEN A NEAT WAY TO FINISH. WHEN IN LONDON DO AS THE GREEKS DO, WHOM
IT SEEMS LET THEIR CHILDREN PLAY NAKED IN THE SUN. MY FAVOURITE
FLOWER-NAME IS SELF-HEAL.

THE SOUND OF FOOTSTEPS UPSTAIRS

Upstairs I hear a floorboard creak and a door close. It is my brother James. He has gone into another room, or The Other Room from the Pink Floyd song, and whether or not I dare speak of things that look like the end of 'Bike' I do not know but it would not be wise to present the evidence I have gleaned from reading. All night I was up and wrote a long poem but I don't know if it should be rendered available for public consumption or not, concerning our rare bird as it does, the red kite. The red kite sailed on the Ally Ally O and said "this is a bit ridiculous, this could go on forever," and surrendered all his toys to the void. Hello.

John Tucker

HANNAH145

Maybe it needs some hens at the end? Would Lyra from Pullman descend from a portal? The media bleat on the telly and the sheep bleat in the field but a bullet up a telegraph pole knows no death and that is the gist of my word-world. I thought I should let you know that when last I turned to my poetry and realised "I have no audience, and a poet needs an audience to survive," then my sister Hannah said "deem it the songs and do it for me." When I say she said that, it was on the Intercom, for she is miles away. I had a dream by the way that I was at a party with her, my sister Hannah; and the epicentre was so exciting and intense in terms of drugs, music, clothes, the party just had to be spread outward, and could only be done so by dancing. It was on waking from that dream and I must remember this too, that Hannah's ideal of keeping rock songs rather than, say, monopolising indigenous wisdom in regimented metres, was the way forward. The only problem I found with this herein was what my father would say: that after so much that might be labelled genius, in action and word, to be another fretboard masturbating songwriter would be a waste; that I have not the natural musical gift to warrant a career in music; that I would be best suited to literature; that it's fair enough if I have musical talent but for me it's just a vapid fashion statement suitable for the rebellion of youth.

THE ACID-CASUALTY VERSION OF SEPTEMBER 11TH

He found himself on a plane.
He found himself on a.
He found himself on.
He found himself.
He found.
P.

John Tucker

147

O TO BE DOSSING IN CAMBRIDGE AGAIN. WE KNEW A MAN CALLED F .R. A. N.
K. WHO SAID "THIS WILL KNOCK YOUR BOLLOCKS OFF LADS," AND "MUSIC
SHOULD BE ALL AROUND US ALL THE TIME." GOING DOWN TO THE DOCTOR
THE SCREEN SAID "IF YOU HAVE A DRUGS PROBLEM TALK TO F. R. A. N. K."
HE WAS AN ACRONYM, THEIR FRANK, OURS A REAL PERSON. OF COURSE SYD
B WAS RUMOURED TO HAVE BEEN SEEN WALKING ROUND WITH A FISH-
STRAPPED TO HIS HEAD. OF COURSE THERE WAS A LAMP-POST CALLED
'REALITY CHECK POINT' WHERE ONCE IF I REMEMBER RIGHTLY I TALKED
ABOUT INJECTING SMACK INTO THE UNIVERSAL MIND THROUGH SNOW
FALL TO SOME HIGHLY ERUDITE STRANGERS. AH YES, HOW COULD I
FORGET, MY STEALING SOOOOOOOO MANY BOOKS FROM BORDERS, AND
MY FRIEND PAUL, WHOM IT SEEMS I WAS DEEPLY IN LOVE WITH, BUILDING
A BONFIRE OF THEM IN THE PUB GARDEN AT NIGHT TO KEEP WARM,
READING OUT A POEM, ASKING "IS IT WORTH BURNING?" BEFORE
FUELLING THE FLAMES. WE DEEM IT THAT THE CHIMNEY IS SMOKING.

THE TOP OF BLACK COMBE

I wonder if there'll ever come a time I break from writing rock songs and start writing, say, songs about sleeping on top of the oldest fell Black Combe on a supportive spring mattress of heather

*

Purple heather beneath the summer weather,
under my body where I lie down,
there is Gore-Tex in my boot of leather,
which I bought away in the town.

I look up at the ancient cinema and see,
the whale from the Natural History Museum fly over,
I eat my popcorn before infinity,
and only wish I was with my lover.

If she was here although there's no-one,
maybe we could make a baby,
there'll be no-one other until the rising of the sun,
we'll have to say yes and not just maybe.

It would be our own Midsummer Night's Dream,
the cosmos is a hole that goes on forever,
the air this time of year would be warm,
and we'd tell our kids we never made it ever!

*

See, I think that would be a fucking excellent song and that I would keep it among the good 'uns if I ever went on a diet and purged the set list of all things crime. It could be a song as good as The Scarecrow by Syd Barrett, although I know we're not to compare ourselves with him. It just goes to show if you know what you're doing it can flow in a matter of five minutes or less. To write the words with a spontaneous melody in your head can also lever the words out more substantially.

John Tucker

NOW I WOULD LOOK DOWN

A few days ago I told myself if I managed to publish a book of song lyrics it would be an amazing opportunity to start a second – to write a whole second song lyric book – from scratch – which is a blank slate situation I for one have not had since I was 14 or 15 and emulating the likes of Cobain. I used to be able to write five or six a day, words and guitar too, with no guitar present, through a notation system I invented, for want of any knowledge of the notes, and which was mostly based on bar-chords. I remember a chorus that went

Little Miss Take,
Little Miss Take,
Little Miss Take,
she's a little mistake.

If that was copying the Mr. Men books we used to read as terribly small children then there were other chorus like

Just another shooting rock star,
Just another shooting rock star,
Just another shooting rock star,
Just another shooting star.

So I was emulating the likes of Cobain. I could also write a poem as I proved in this period in the example of 'The Fire-dance' [now set to music] but mostly it was anti- poetry I was writing. Any old seemingly witty word-play could become a chorus like

I'm having an art attack,
I'm having an art attack,
no worse than a heart attack,
I'm having an art attack.

These were the days my mnemonic was Even A Dick Gets Big Erections which I deem to be punk. By the way I almost found a better mnemonic for the strings the other day but like most dream women it got away. Anyhow, what I was meaning to say was it is good to look to the future sometimes and plan ahead. To start again with a blank slate and make a second song book could see me cure a lot of boredom and kill a lot of time – as Michael Hofmann says process time to trial and outcome.

In fact I would be soooooooooo excited to start a second life as a dreamer and doodler with a musical edge that I think my headache about what to publish is now assuaged: it has to be the present, not a collection of words that have no melodies or guitar parts. The dream of having a blank slate to do it all again – or rather to do it all differently - to build on the first – is a beautiful dream of freedom I have not had for a while.

Soundcloud Rain

DEATH TO THE FINGERTIP DANCER

B/t/w/ there was a time the 4 solo albums posited herein were actual albums on Soundcloud I mean Bandcamp but I took them down and the book just stayed in the same shape it was when they were there

and was added to a little bit

re-jigged finetuned tempered doctored andcetera

and as I write there are a bunch of songs on the Soundcloud account of John F B Tucker – which I consider to be demo quality only. Just me overlaying a slick, processed beat with 2 electrics and a vocal, leaving a big bass-shaped hole, it's New Beat, amateur-and-proud, DIY, lo-fi, bedroom music.

The Flood's 6-song algorithm is still on Soundcloud under the rhythm guitarist Tom Woodhall's name.

Black Hole Myths (formerly Funnelspirals) have music online too but it's only music, it's not exactly death, the death of a loved one, or a scientific breakthrough, or a meal for a starving family.

It is music and only music, solipsistic in listening and telepathic or even co-imaginative in playing. It is penetration of is-ness; and meaning in it is faces in the fire or Hamlet's three creatures in a cloud-change – but it's not neuro-science.

It's a cryptic crossword puzzle to some extent.

It's made of waves!

Ah, what do I know. I know next to nothing about it really. I could tell you what Dr. Ptom Fitzgerald says though – 'Born Slippy' is evidence dance can have a soul. Oasis is good for bittersweet, comedown energy. The G note is green on the fretboard. We had some conversations, some demeanours when we were young. I could show you a poem from that time – sweet 16 – that sees me aping Jim Morrison's The Lords And The New Creatures if you want… okay.

John Tucker

NECKLACE NOOSE

I

Necklace noose,
reckless truce,
drooling before

wet, electric eyes...

ii

a salmon escaped the ancient net.
A sprightly hypertext sniper on
Piper At The Gates Of Dawn
accrued to the procession.
The anguila eel is wet and
named after the devil for
mysteriously appearing in
the puddles of towns on rainy days.

iii

Literature is a vehicle. Punk
is an attitude more than a
genre of music. Piggy
is a symbol of Reason and
dies. Civilisation is but a
thin veneer belied by dark,
arational forces. The doors film
is emblematic of a paranoid
meltdown into post-euphoric
psychosis. Yeah, dance music
can have a soul for sure.

iv

A purple parrot perched upon the
shoulder of the pirate squawking
"don't tell Moronika." A green
one was sent to space through
the conch... maybe all I need
is a length of metal chain. A Lion
Bar was driven through the economy
in a car and a carfume whooshed
from the unicorn's bottom...

v

Soundcloud Rain

and why did the chicken cross
the road if not to break on
through to the Other Side,
break on through to the Other
Side, break on through to the
Other Side? I am the Burger
King, I can eat anything.
Preferably a Double Whopper
with cheese, fries and a Coke.

Vi

When 'The End' is playing
on the jukebox I can clear up
the pool balls, when the boys
are away on holiday, and
the noose lets us go, and
thinking I can drink more
firewater whisky than I can
I puke on the carpet when
the boys get home, when
we are new you and new me.

(1998 reconstructed)

John Tucker

Ah yes those were the days I used to play Happy Birthday on a 30 CM ruler bent over a physics desk at varying lengths and wobbled

those were the days I used to teach myself how to play things like Prodigy 'Poison' on the organic drums

days I remember all my knife that I used to touch the unplugged electric to the large wooden structure of the bunk bed and amplify it organically

those were days of first going to Glastonbury

of first getting osteopathy

of liking grunge and indie

and reading the NME

and I wonder what happened to it all

London and lust and looking good

did it all become dust

and did we know it would?

Soundcloud Rain

CONTAINMENT

The black dude sitting on the bench in the park in London is playing the same as me

a new presence enters the room at the end of the song or it should do for free

the soft A is open, the G is gold, the F for fucking then the G's colour has changed

the smouldering sunset wants to smoke pollen with Paul and set our senses rearranged

I'm smuggling my squidgy black through customs on the conscious/ unconscious border

if I may again be the young lion I would not do anything that leads to a psychotic disorder

summer smudges my lucidity as we float on an endless sea might never be back again

above the park the angels on CCTV look down from the tree which a dream might contain

to keep the meaning dreaming and the dream contained I pause for thought for a century

I forget just why I smell bubblegum whenever I choose but I guess it's just me

TRADING ANGEL AFFIRMATIONS

What do you do
with a literary failure
what do you do
with a literary failure
what do you do
with a literary failure
early in the morning?

Woke up this morning
feeling so bad
felt like a pig
had shat in my head

He-Man's out to get me
that's the way it seems
people always let you down

so do those that die
for no hamburger heaven
draw the same as those
that shape 9/ 11?

and don't forget a rose
would smell as sweet
if it were but called
barmy as the army of
Michael Vaughan, m' Lord,
Michael Vaughan, Michael
Vaughan m' Lord,
Michael Vaughan, Michael
Vaughan, m' Lord,
Michael Vaughan

yeah yeah yeah you're
in the broken army
now broken army

well it's a one for the money,
money for the blow,
blow to get hairy now
go cat go but don't you
silence my cosmic Muse

do they know it's
my 40th birthday
tomorrow at all?

Lean in your tits
when I'm sitting in Kutz

Soundcloud Rain

with my hair everywhere
like a malting scarecrow

chicken korma police
arrest this man
he talks in curry

to be very blunt
Aphex acid isn't flaccid

ecstasia so much
to answer for

my childhood won't smile,
my childhood won't smile,
but I'm gonna be big

feeeeeeeeed the
biiiiiiiiiiirds
let them know
it's my birthday tomorrow

God save the queen
we mean it man
her Hitler hairdo
is making me feel ill
and we have crashed
her party everybody
must get stoned

close your eyes
make it a better place
for you and for me
and the entire human race

suicide is dangerous
it brings on many changes

liquid donkey
liquid donkey
tra la la la la la la

I am the Almighty Cornholio
and I bring you water
water when you touch me
water when you
hold me tight

poetry it's over
poetry away
poetry or not
as the case may be

John Tucker

somewhere over the
fractured acid-rainbow
Baxter the dog flies

teenage mutant
ganja turtles heroes
in a halfshell
Turtle Power!

Soundcloud Rain

Back in the day the best Flood gig was when Niki (or Agent G aka Wolf) and I tuned up, warmed up, and then there was a power cut. It was no accident it was the gig. The whole warehouse went black for minutes and when the lights came back on that was it, we had performed already. We really did push the boundaries as to what could be a song, even more so than the guy that moved rocks about in a river to change its pitch, or the guy that destroyed a table with an axe. Our songs had a psychotechnological edge. If you consider poetry as a defamiliarisation of perception – if you also consider Rimbaud's comment that the poet makes himself a visionary through a prodigious derangement of the senses to attain the unknown – then the very act of recording through earphones was a poetic act in itself. I think that night when we presented a power-cut as music there was one band on after us and they played and played until their fingers were sore and their frontman ended up down on the floor, writhing about, screaming lyrics into the mic. That seems to be what I have been doing herein, in a way, in the sense of having run out of lyrics a while back and still carrying on.

The reason it is being a book and not only a new-look net-book on my blog on the bot is that nobody reads it when it's on the bot – for maybe it's too long for that - and what I want is a literary career or at least a chance to score.

My dad wouldn't mind this book going out there.

It's like we needed to create our own website.

It's like the book I wrote at seven – did I mention it? - that predicted the net and which got stolen – it's being replaced.

I tell myself that if I were bringing a poem collection out - I tell myself there is enough contained within to satisfy that desire and both birds are killed with one stone.

Signed by everwell, she couldn't hit it sideways, or maybe a soothsaying Spiderman with the hairgel of Dracula, Atlantis, Aquarius, the 60's.

www.ingramcontent.com/pod-product-compliance
Lightning Source LLC
Chambersburg PA
CBHW022056050726
47591CB00002B/563